The Future of Work

Trends, Opportunities, and Threats in 2020 and Beyond

Jack Spain

The Future of Work – Trends, Opportunities, and Threats in 2020 and Beyond

Publisher: **Spain Business Advisors**

Editor: Chris Duke
Cover Design: Adarsh Kiran Narayanadas

Copyright   © 2019 Spain Business Advisors

All rights reserved

Printed in the United States of America

No part of this publication may be reproduced, stored in or introduced into a retrieval system, or transmitted, in any form, or by any means (electronic, mechanical, photo-copying, recording or otherwise), without the prior permission of the author. Requests for permission should be directed to jack <at> jackspain.com.

1st Edition – December 2019

   ISBN: 9781707623426
   1. Work
   2. Jobs
   3. Careers
   4. Recruitment
   5. Future

Spain Business Advisors
Cary, NC USA
jack <at> jackspain.com
https://www.linkedin.com/in/jackspain/

DEDICATION

To my exceptionally amazing and accomplished daughters, nieces, and nephews. Each of you have chosen remarkable professional careers and have already and will continue to make extraordinary contributions in your respective vocations. I am extraordinarily proud of each of you and am blessed to have you in my life. I wish you incredible success and fulfilment in your individual career pursuits and adventures.

Much of my research during the past several months was inspired also by pondering the future for my beautiful young grandnieces who will be embarking on their own interesting personal career journeys in two decades. I pray that they will have the opportunity to explore and engage in inspiring and fulfilling careers and life experiences of their own during the remainder of this century and beyond.

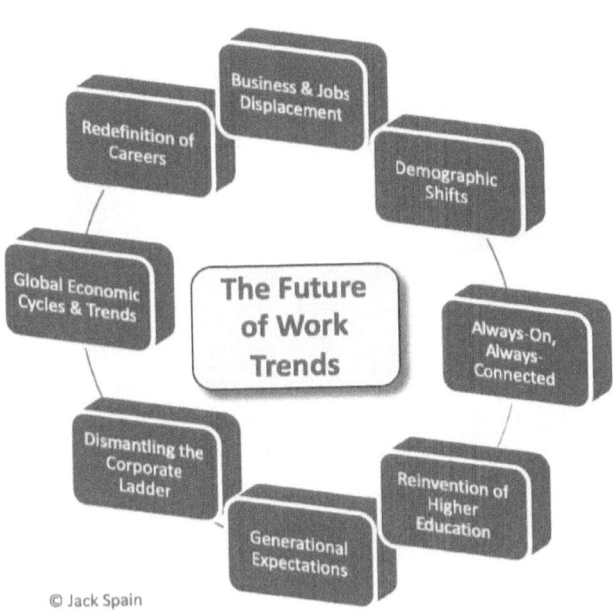

The Future of Work

CONTENTS

DEDICATION III
CONTENTS VII
ACKNOWLEDGMENTS I
FORWARD 1
PREFACE 11
CONTEMPLATING THE FUTURE OF WORK 13
ACCELERATED BUSINESS AND JOBS DISPLACEMENT ... 17
DEMOGRAPHIC SHIFTS 31
ALWAYS-ON, ALWAYS-CONNECTED WORLD 43
REINVENTION OF HIGHER EDUCATION 47
GENERATIONAL EXPECTATIONS 59
GLOBAL ECONOMIC CYCLES AND TRENDS 65
DISMANTLING THE CORPORATE LADDER 77
REDEFINING THE CONCEPT OF A CAREER 81
CONCLUSIONS AND RECOMMENDATIONS 89
    GUIDANCE FOR JOB SEEKERS 91
    GUIDANCE FOR EMPLOYERS 94
    GUIDANCE FOR RECRUITING & TALENT ACQUISITION PROFESSIONALS . 98
ABOUT THE AUTHOR 105
ENDNOTES 109

ACKNOWLEDGMENTS

I would like to acknowledge my immediate and extended family members who have provided me with remarkable insights during the past several decades along with my digital native colleagues who have opened my mind to our new modern world of work. I have also been fortunate with opportunities to mentor a number of younger professionals over the past several decades who have inspired me and rewarded me with tremendous insights into careers, work, priorities, relationships, family, and life.

I would like to express my appreciation to my former colleagues from the Leoforce Marketing team who have provided support and encouragement to research this topic and to share my insights with others.

Once again, I am pleased to have the opportunity to express my sincere gratitude to Chris Duke, a successful serial entrepreneur and one of the most interesting and imaginative thinkers that I have ever known. Chris has been an inspiration to me for two decades, sharing his passion, creativity, compassion, and resourcefulness. He has also been a constant and faithful sounding board on numerous business, technology, entrepreneurial, career, and life topics. He is certainly one of the most talented storytellers and writers that I have ever met, and I continue to enjoy our frequent interactions on a very diverse set of fascinating topics.

FORWARD

I grew up in a household with parents whose employment environment is, for all practical purposes, extinct. At least in the United States. There are certainly a few jobs that still pay out full pensions and healthcare for life, but I can't imagine someone entering the workforce today will find those options at any company, large or small.

When Jack shared his research and asked me to reflect on my work experience, it was an opportunity to revisit my journey in a different way. To review the story and to think again about the signposts I encountered along the way. In Jack's book, he shares a wealth of insights that can be viewed as signposts for what the work journey might be for you, your company and the next generations entering the workforce. For anyone that has ever traveled beyond your local comfort zone, you know the importance of paying attention to the signs that help you reach your destination.

For as long as I can remember, my Mom and Dad both worked for General Electric at Appliance Park in Louisville, Kentucky. Mom was an engineer working in management and Dad was a member of the union, working in the factory. With the exception of my Dad taking odd jobs during an extended strike, I can't remember my parents ever considering any other employment. We had nothing but GE appliances in our home. We attended GE sponsored events like Family Day at Kings Island amusement park. My Junior Achievement company in high school was sponsored by, you guessed it, General Electric.

As the child of a GE employee, we were eligible for summer employment at Appliance Park. I worked there one summer during my college years and it marked one of my earliest revelations about what work I would likely pursue. I don't remember exactly what I was paid per hour, but I do remember thinking that as a college student, this was a fortune.

I was treated well during my time there. The work was not hard, but it was repetitive, monotonous and offered little mental stimulation other

The Future of Work

than watching the cast of characters at the plant, some of whom I am certain spent most of their adult life there.

I'm grateful for the opportunity and for what General Electric provided my family. But it was clear to me at that point that working in a factory on an assembly line was not in my long-term employment plan.

After graduating from high school, I headed off to college with a general idea of what I might want to do for work. My experience in Junior Achievement fueled my passion for business and started me down that path. While Kentucky Wesleyan College is a liberal arts school, I focused my studies around business, graduating with a BA and a double major in Accounting and Management.

Like many college students, I held a variety of small jobs, each of which exerted a small measure of influence into how I'd ultimately pursue work. Places I worked included a law firm, a convenience store, and as a bouncer in an under-21 nightclub started by a couple of friends from Owensboro.

But perhaps my most influential work during college was an internship at IBM in Evansville, Indiana. It was there where I got my first taste of working in a professional office, interacting with executives, salespeople, support engineers and other staff. It was more than a job; it was like working with a family. It was where I learned what it feels like to work in an environment that is both competitive and nurturing at the same time. This was another milestone or signpost.

I supported the sales folks in the office and remember a time when one of the salespeople was not going to make her quota. Our office covered a geographic area in Southern Indiana and Western Kentucky. Our branch manager, Buzz Koenig, called in all the salespeople for a meeting and announced that everyone was going to make quota and we were going to help the one salesperson who was not making quota. The entire team spent time in her territory, as a group, until enough was sold enough to make her quota. It was a powerful lesson about succeeding as a team, as a family.

The Future of Work

When I graduated, I hoped to find a home at IBM. But alas, they were in a hiring freeze. Buzz made a phone call and helped me land an offer at Mead Johnson Pharmaceuticals in their sales department. I had an offer to be an accountant. I stood at the crossroads and took the turn toward sales, leading me to North Carolina.

After working in sales for a couple of years, I once again felt the tug to go back and learn more about business. I applied to MBA programs in North Carolina and managed to land an attractive offer from Duke University's Fuqua School of Business. I'm not sure if my last name helped with the application process, but it certainly did not exclude me from paying tuition as I am not a member of that Duke family. But I did land a nice scholarship from Junior Achievement that made the next leg of figuring out my life's work a little more affordable.

As a fulltime student at Fuqua, I had the opportunity to take all the experiences of my work life and put them to work in my studies. I worked small jobs to help cover expenses (like stacking produce at the Wellspring Grocery in Durham), but did not have the burden of working a full time job and trying to learn about business from so many different angles. This was a unique time in life when I had the opportunity to think about how work might look for me in the future.

It was a magical time to be at Fuqua. The school made the Top 10 Business School list for the first time. Our class was filled with a culturally diverse and incredibly bright group of students from around the globe. Some have gone on to tremendous financial success and at least one has achieved global recognition for her charitable foundation, Melinda Gates of the Bill and Melinda Gates Foundation.

During my time there, it seemed that a majority of the students were focused on landing jobs in banking and finance. Recruitment days when investment banks came to campus created a sea of dark suits and crisp white shirts or blouses. But there were a few of us who opted to pursue a different path.

One of my friends combined his love of music with a desire to start a record label for up and coming artists. Instead of suiting up for interviews, Jay spent his time in clubs listening to bands and figuring

The Future of Work

out how to apply what he was learning to the business of music. After graduation, he gave birth to Mammoth Records that was eventually sold to Disney Music Group.

I was in an entrepreneurship class during my last semester. Our group was working on external cabinet designs for personal computers. We wanted them to look more stylish than the plain putty color. After a chance meeting with a classmate and a couple of sessions of ideas on a napkin, my two other classmates and I decided to start a company selling wooden cabinet enclosures for computers. More than simply a startup or a job, this was another key signpost I followed that led me to where I am today.

With a healthy round of seed funding from a classmate, we built prototypes around the IBM PC and the Apple Macintosh. As freshly minted MBAs, we started our business with grand hopes for making an impact on the computer market. We found a manufacturer, called on stores, went to trade shows and did all the things we had trained for to make this company a success.

But we did not have the Internet in 1987. Computer designs continued to change at a rapid pace, and while everyone (including Steve Jobs at Macworld one year) thought our products looked fantastic, the sales simply did not come. After a couple of years, we ran out of our seed money and decided to shut down the company.

At this point, my 'work experience suitcase' was reasonably diverse and my diploma collection complete, at least to the Masters level. I thought of going out to the corporate world and finding my next work experience, but there was something about having my own company that I just could not shake.

I headed back to Kentucky and re-connected with two of my closest friends from high school. We kicked around some ideas and before we knew it, we decided to start a company. I'd describe it as a collage, with consulting, fund raising, computers, software and a chain of hair salons all mashed together. In hindsight the outcome was obvious, but at the time it all seemed to make sense. I can still remember the words from

The Future of Work

one of my partners when he said, "What's the worst that can happen? We go bankrupt and start over." It was fortuitous.

We did manage to gain some initial traction. The salon company opened a couple of locations and the software side of the business started selling desktop applications. We added computer sales, networking and custom development to our repertoire. It was the early 1990's and without question, I saw that the future of work for me clearly included something in the rapidly evolving computer technology. I would put this in the category of a major milestone for me.

But alas, after several years of struggling to generate enough revenue to cover overly opulent office space and equipment, the business was forced to cease operations. As the president and guarantor for the majority of company debt, I received my PhD in what happens when a business spends more than they make. It was indeed painful, but there is some value in starting work all over again, on the ground floor.

At this point, I was ready to start fresh, leaving behind my years of sleeping on friend's couches, borrowing cars and living off credit cards. I was ready to re-enter the work world and find a new path that allowed me to use my practical experience, my formal learning and the shirtsleeve wisdom I'd picked up along the way.

Working in some area of technology was how I viewed the future of my work at the time. I landed a job selling computers and software at a CAD company owned by a friend's family. Not only did I find my financial footing, I had the opportunity to again get a taste of what I first experienced at IBM. Yes, it was a commission job selling computers and software, but it was also a family environment where we all supported each other.

After a couple years of success at selling computers and software, I had the opportunity to head back to North Carolina and enter the world of technology consulting. I started in professional services for a large ComputerLand franchise. This led to a progression of roles at three other technology companies in a variety of professional service, consulting and project management roles. In each case, I made

The Future of Work

deposits in my work experience bank account while the wounds of my early adventures in entrepreneurship continued to heal and fade.

My experiences in the world of technology sales and consulting had a profound impact on my view of what 'work' actually is. When I was at GE, my work was making sure that the panel on the front of that model of range had two screws and all the wires were connected. My experiences over the past 10 years of work, entrepreneurship and academics gave me a different perspective of how what we call 'work' plays into the flow of business, and life.

My first leap into the new world of technology known as the Internet came in 1999. I joined a startup called SciQuest. I arrived a few weeks before their IPO, too late for any 'Friends and Family' stock benefits, but early enough in the process to ride the wave. And what a ride it was.

Just as my work experience for the prior 10 years had shifted dramatically from my days on the assembly line at GE, the next four years would represent another quantum shift in how I viewed work. To begin with, things happened fast. I mean really fast. SciQuest was working to change business processes in ways that had never been done before. It felt as if we were laying track a few hundred yards ahead of a charging locomotive.

My experience growing up was that a part of taking a job was your title. You worked for that and held on to it for years, perhaps decades. I had seven titles in four years at SciQuest, all in different areas of the company. When something new came up that needed doing, I'd raise my hand and say, 'yes, I can do that'.

As you might expect of a company moving that fast in uncharted territory, eventually, we ran out of space to lay that track, coming to a chasm that could not be easily crossed given the payload of employees, technology, facilities, etc. It started with a 10% cut across the board. This was not nearly enough as more followed.

I believe we reached a peak of around 450 people. By the time I made the decision to step off the train (yes – it was my decision) there were

The Future of Work

about 90 of us left. It was an incredible ride filled with joy, sorrow and pain. Once again, my view of work forever changed.

Prior to SciQuest's decline, my wife and I had started a side gig. No direct relation to technology. After winning Grand Champion in a cheesecake bake-off at SciQuest with my Apple Bourbon Cheesecake, I was finally convinced that I should sell the product.

Pulling from my suitcase of experience, we started the company off on the right foot. We incorporated, got permits, licenses, inspections and everything required. Rather than go all in making a load of products to start, I found one customer, the chef at a local restaurant. He bought one cheesecake. Then another, then two more. He gave us feedback and we learned along the way. I asked a lot of questions and sought out those who had similar work experience.

We grew the business on the side until finally, in 2003, I felt we had enough business and cash in the bank to take a leap of faith. I walked into my manager's office, raised my arm as if pulling the cord to ring the bell on a streetcar, and said, 'It's time for me to get off the bus'.

Anna's Gourmet Goodies has grown steadily since that time. We started in the wholesale dessert business, but after reaching maximum capacity with our facilities and equipment, decided to pivot to the cookie gift business. We found we could produce lower volumes at much higher margin than the wholesale business. And by combining my technology skills with better than average baking skills, have carved out a niche as an online retailer with extensive technical capabilities to serve a variety of customer needs.

The path of work that I have followed is anything but a straight line. When I crossed the stage to get my diploma from Moore High School, I can say with certainty that I was not prepared to predict the future of my work as it exists today. And I believe that, despite having access to the most awe-inspiring technology in the history of mankind, combined with the smartest minds on the planet, that predicting the exact location of where you will be 10, 20 or 30 years in the future is simply not possible.

The Future of Work

We can, however, use what we are learning as signposts to help plan and prepare for a future that will no doubt exceed anything we can imagine. The research and framework from Jack's book serve as a reference guide of signposts we can use to navigate the complexities of not only how we will work, but how it will impact the evolution of our daily lives. As the white lines on a highway pass by us faster and faster as our speed increases, we must pay closer attention to what is happening in our work environments as the pace of technology continues to accelerate.

Here are some things I've learned that, combined with the research in this book, can help guide your work journey.

Create Value

Ultimately, every type of work we perform is about creating value. Sometimes it is about monetary value in goods and services. Sometimes it is about creating value for all of humankind when we volunteer to help others. And sometimes it is emotional value for ourselves. As human beings we all seek to find our purpose on Earth. Doing work that is of some value is an important component of being human.

Solve Problems

Businesses exist because they solve a problem of some kind. Or they fill a need. If there is no problem or no need, it is unlikely that any business will survive for long. Remember, you cannot solve any problem unless you identify it first.

Acquire Skills

It is difficult to find any report or listen to any news story about the economy, business, jobs, etc. these days without hearing the universal cry from a majority of employers, 'We can't find enough people with the right skills to fill jobs'. This is most certainly true, but the real question we need to ask is 'Why?'.

The Future of Work

Barriers to information required to learn virtually anything are practically zero. Search engines have solved the problem of access to information. What is needed is a focus on changing the desire to acquire these skills. Cloud computing, artificial intelligence, data warehousing, are all wonderful tools. But they require real work to master. And to master anything, you must be willing to learn new skills.

My daughter is on the verge of graduating from college with her BA. For most of her life, she's grown up in a family where our work was building and operating Anna's Gourmet Goodies. Her degree will focus on nutrition and exercise science, but like most college students, she is wrestling with how to start her work journey post college.

Fortunately, she has worked a variety of jobs, adding valuable deposits into her work experience bank account. And she has seen, up-close and firsthand, the ins and outs, ups and downs of running a small business.

I am confident that Anna will not join a company with unlimited benefits, a full pension and lifetime employment. Instead I expect her to weave together a patchwork of jobs and experiences that hopefully include a mix of my experience in the three areas mentioned earlier.

The work landscape for Anna will change in ways that it is not possible for me to imagine, even in my wildest dreams. Less than 100 years ago, her grandmother was born into a home without indoor plumbing, running water or electricity. Transportation happened via walking or if they were lucky, a horse drawn cart. It's not lost on me that I sit here, connected to the entire world via the Internet and can, with a few keystrokes, access many times more information than even existed from the dawn of history to the time when my mother was born.

When I think about the future of work, I think of transformation. It will be a fast-paced and complex transformation. One of my favorite quotes on transformation comes from my friend, author and speaker August Turak.

"When you give a thirsty man a drink, you transform his condition. When a poor man wins the lottery, you

The Future of Work

transform his circumstances. But when Mr. Scrooge wakes up on Christmas morning, he has a transformation of being."

It is this final transformation that is my hope for Anna and other generations to come.

Despite the uncertainties of our times, I remain hopeful that Anna and her generation will learn from our experiences, watch the signposts, and forge new paths that will be just as spectacular as they would be for my mother if she were here today. It will happen. Time to get to work.

Chris Duke
Co-Founder, Anna's Gourmet Goodies

The Future of Work

PREFACE

The concept for this book was inspired by a rather eclectic and disparate array of sources. For the past thirty-five years I have been an avid reader – primarily on business, leadership, management, entrepreneurial, change management, product management, sales, marketing, and technology topics. During the past several years I have introduced a variety of science, historical, biographical, and fiction works that have continued to educate and enlighten me. Like some people I know, I am guilty of subscribing to far too many blogs, email newsletters, news media sources, and podcasts – but they continue to fuel my natural intellectual curiosity about all things and provide me with intriguing daily insights into our world.

As I dug deeper into this topic, I imagined myself writing a couple of blog posts to share with our Marketing team. Those posts morphed into additional topics and blog posts, which triggered a considerable amount of additional research and ultimately a research paper. Once I reached that point, I felt compelled to organize my findings and insights in another book to publish.

This project began in the spring of 2019 and this topic has inspired me to continue on this journey to contemplate the future of work and the ultimate impact on my children, extended family members, friends, and colleagues. We stand at the cusp of incredible shifts in how, why, where, and how much we work. This book is only the beginning of my pursuit on this topic and I hope that you will find the inspiration to join me on this journey as well.

The Future of Work

The Future of Work

CONTEMPLATING THE FUTURE OF WORK

"Without ambition one starts nothing. Without work one finishes nothing. The prize will not be sent to you. You have to win it."

— *Ralph Waldo Emerson*

I believe we are currently experiencing seismic changes on multiple fronts as we approach another new decade in the 21st century. As the pace of change continues to accelerate exponentially from decade to decade, it becomes increasingly challenging to predict the types of career and job opportunities that will be available in the next five to ten years, let alone the decades beyond. Much of what constitutes our jobs today did not exist five to ten years ago.

My research on this topic ultimately uncovered eight key trends that provide insights into the future of work that will affect all of us.

Accelerated Business and Jobs Displacement. Internet-based business disintermediation (reduction in the use of intermediaries between producers and consumers) that occurred in a big way in the mid-1990s along with technological advances like big data analytics, Natural Language Processing (NLP), Artificial Intelligence (AI), deep machine learning, neural networks, behavioral pattern analytics, and predictive analytics have spawned new digital business models which are compressing company lifecycles and triggering massive displacements of both businesses and jobs.

Demographic Shifts. We are undergoing considerable demographic shifts that impact the workforce and resource planning including an increasing number of Baby Boomer retirements, higher penetration of women in the workplace, decreasing birth rates in conjunction with a delay in childbearing ages, and increasing lifespans for younger

The Future of Work

workers.

Always-On, Always-Connected World. New mobile and wearable technologies along with innovative collaboration and social media platforms have led to the establishment of a 24 x 7 x 365 "always-on" world. These innovations continue to collapse geographic boundaries across the globe. The introduction of coworking and shared spaces has also been challenging the necessity of common physical workspaces for collaboration and the concept of a standard workday. Introduction of 5G technology infrastructure and 5G devices in the next several years will intensify the impact of this trend.

Reinvention of Higher Education. I believe that a major transformation is underway for our institutions of learning. While standard curriculums for core science and liberal arts education will likely continue indefinitely, the impact of each of the major paradigm shifts underway will especially challenge higher education institutions to reinvent themselves in order to continue to be relevant to the increasingly rapidly changing business and workforce requirements. This trend will also have a dramatic impact on how employers continue to develop and nurture a culture of continuous training and learning within their institutions.

Generational Expectations. Employers currently struggle with generational differences relative to the expectations of work and the workplace in order to stay relevant, especially in our current hyper-competitive talent market. I have personally witnessed rather notable changes in the workplace over the past several decades and can only assume that generational-related expectations will continue to be a key workplace opportunity and challenge.

Global Economic Cycles and Trends. We are currently enjoying an extended period of economic growth that has had a very positive impact for many individuals relative to job opportunities. At the same time there are increasing debates about the distribution of wealth across the globe. Furthermore, the introduction of the Internet and other technological advances have created a labor market paradigm shift often referred to as the new gig economy with a prevalence of employment options that include short-term contract or freelance work as opposed to permanent job positions.

Dismantling the Corporate Ladder. As a result of numerous technological advances, the introduction of a multi-stage life for the workforce (explained in additional detail in subsequent chapters) and decreasing institutional lifecycles, I believe that the paradigm of a traditional corporate ladder will be dismantled in the decades ahead. These trends will challenge businesses and institutions to reformulate their concept of organizational structures and the development of leadership talent.

Redefining the Concept of a Career. My recent research has led me to conclude that our concept and framework for a professional career is likely to undergo dramatic changes throughout the decades ahead. Many experts suggest that a majority of the career opportunities that will exist towards the end of the approaching decade have not yet been invented which makes it increasingly challenging for both educational institutions and employers to anticipate the skills requirements for their current and next generation employees. The impact on the workforce will be just as dramatic and individuals will continuously have to anticipate skills and educational credentials requirements to remain gainfully employed.

In the following chapters we'll examine the impact of these potentially seismic paradigm shifts on individuals, businesses, recruiting and talent acquisition professionals. In these chapters I will introduce evidence that I have discovered during my research and offer observations and reflections on these macro trends. I confess that my research has resulted in surfacing more questions than answers for which I will continue to seek greater insight in the years ahead.

While many of the statistics and references included in this book are focused on the United States, I believe that the majority of these trends apply to modern economies across the globe and ultimately impact the concept of work and life across the globe.

ACCELERATED BUSINESS AND JOBS DISPLACEMENT

"Regardless. I think the next 30 years are going to be the most interesting in human history to date. And, I think they are going to be very different than anything we currently anticipate."

— Brad Feld, feld.com, 03-Jun-2019

"Your competitors probably won't come from within your industry—they could come from any industry, or from one that doesn't exist yet."

— James McQuivey, *Digital Disruption: Unleashing the Next Wave of Innovation*

"The biggest impediment to a company's future success is its past success."

— Dan Schulman | CEO of PayPal

■ Observations:

We have witnessed considerable business and jobs displacements over the past two decades as evidenced by:

1. Increasing compression of company lifecycles;
2. Continued supply chain disintermediation (i.e. reduction in the use of intermediaries between producers and consumers) from new Internet and digital-based business models;
3. Rapid advances in the application of robotics and automation technologies; and
4. Application of Artificial Intelligence (AI) methods and technologies across all business and enterprise functions

within both business-to-business (B2B) and business-to-consumer (B2C) industries.

Despite this displacement trend, there also has been encouraging news from a jobs and employment perspective in 2019.

→ **The Evidence:**

- "The U.S. is officially in its longest expansion, breaking the record of 120 months of economic growth from March 1991 to March 2001, according to the National Bureau of Economic Research". [1]
- "There are more jobs than people out of work, something the American economy has never experienced before." [2]
- "Close to 10,000 baby boomers hit age 65 every day." [3]

In conjunction with robust dynamics of supply and demand in the job market, other trends that have emerged over the past few years include:

- "Research shows that since 2000, 52 percent of companies in the Fortune 500 have either gone bankrupt, been acquired, or ceased to exist as a result of digital disruption. The collision of the physical and digital worlds has affected every dimension of society, commerce, enterprises, and individuals." [4]
- "New digital business models are the principal reason why just over half of the names of companies on the Fortune 500 have disappeared since the year 2000". [5]
- "The chances that a small business will survive for five years in the United States are about 35%. But the individuals who open such businesses do not believe that the statistics apply to them". [6]
- "New ecosystems will emerge with significant sectoral changes. There will be substantial changes in who people work for. A century ago, the average life of an S&P 500 company was 67 years. By 2013, it had reduced to 15 years. In other words, people live longer but companies die sooner (not that the two things are necessarily related)." [7]

The Future of Work

- "'50 percent of the companies in this room won't exist in a decade,' he said. 'For you startups, 70 percent of you will fail.' The coming AI revolution is going to bring transition – and not everyone will survive. 'You haven't seen anything in terms of what's about to occur,' he said. 'When you combine artificial intelligence with the Internet of Things, with digitization of companies, with states and businesses – the transformation is going to be tremendous… and it's going to be brutal.'" [8]
- "The disruptive force of technology is killing off older companies earlier and at a much faster rate than decades ago, squeezing employees, investors and other stakeholders, according to a new report… We argue that disruption is nothing new but that the speed, complexity and global nature of it is," the report says. 'In fact, it is clear that a number of sectors are currently impacted by multiple disruptive forces simultaneously.'" [9]
- "Our review of the evidence leads us to conclude that, among the factors whose effects we are able to quantify, labor demand factors are the most important drivers of the secular decline in employment over the 1999 to 2018 period. In this category, the effects of increased imports from China are the single largest contributor to the decline in employment, potentially accounting for an estimated 0.92 percentage point decline in the employment-to-population ratio. The next largest contributor we are able to quantify is the growing penetration of robots into the labor market. Based on the evidence reviewed, we attribute a decline in the employment-to-population ratio of 0.43 percentage point to this factor." [10]
- "Automation, robots and artificial intelligence are having an arguably transformative effect on labor markets in the United States and perhaps in many other advanced economies. Robots, in particular industrial robots, are anticipated to spread rapidly in the next several decades and assume tasks previously performed by labor. These momentous changes are accompanied by concerns about the future of jobs and wages." [11]
- "Heliogen, a clean energy company that emerged from stealth mode on Tuesday, said it has discovered a way to use artificial

intelligence and a field of mirrors to reflect so much sunlight that it generates extreme heat above 1,000 degrees Celsius. Essentially, Heliogen created a solar oven — one capable of reaching temperatures that are roughly a quarter of what you'd find on the surface of the sun. The breakthrough means that, for the first time, concentrated solar energy can be used to create the extreme heat required to make cement, steel, glass and other industrial processes. In other words, carbon-free sunlight can replace fossil fuels in a heavy carbon-emitting corner of the economy that has been untouched by the clean energy revolution." [12]

- "Battery prices, which were above $1,100 per kilowatt-hour in 2010, have fallen 87% in real terms to $156/kWh in 2019. By 2023, average prices will be close to $100/kWh, according to the latest forecast from research company BloombergNEF (BNEF). Cost reductions in 2019 are thanks to increasing order size, growth in battery electric vehicle sales and the continued penetration of high energy density cathodes. The introduction of new pack designs and falling manufacturing costs will drive prices down in the near term. BNEF's 2019 Battery Price Survey, published today at the BNEF Summit in Shanghai, predicts that as cumulative demand passes 2TWh in 2024, prices will fall below $100/kWh. This price is seen as the point around which EVs will start to reach price parity with internal combustion engine vehicles." [13]
- "Based on the tasks that workers perform, Frey and Osborne (2013), for instance, classify 702 occupations by how susceptible they are to automation. They conclude that over the next two decades, 47 percent of US workers are at risk of automation. Using a related methodology, McKinsey puts the same number at 45 percent, while the World Bank estimates that 57 percent of jobs in the OECD could be automated over the next two decades (World Development Report, 2016)." [14]
- "A.I. specialist, is the fastest growing U.S. job in terms of number of hires, at least according to LinkedIn, which published its annual emerging jobs report on Tuesday. Hirings for A.I. specialists on the career networking service have grown 74% annually over the past four years, LinkedIn

The Future of Work

said. But it didn't reveal how many jobs that represents, only that demand for that job role is growing faster than other emerging jobs. ... No. 2 on the list was 'robotics engineer,' an umbrella term for both physical robotics and so-called robotic process automation, a trendier technology that involves software automating basic tasks like entering data into a table. The third fastest growing job in terms of hiring was 'data scientist.'" [15]

- "Cubicle workers. Shipping clerks. Loan processors. 'All gone,' Forrester vice president and principal consultant Huard Smith said in describing the impact of artificial intelligence on various professions by 2030. Smith's list included a lot of repetitive, manual work that can be automated with machine-learning software. For instance, Forrester projects that 73% of all cubicle-related jobs—think clerical tasks like data entry—will be automated by 2030, equating to over 20 million jobs eliminated. Location-based workers, which includes people who work as grocery store clerks, will also be severely impacted by A.I., Smith explained. About 38% of location-based jobs will be automated by 2030, eliminating about 29.9 million positions." [16]

- "U.S. diners spent almost $27 billion last year ordering food for delivery by app, website or text message, according to the NPD Group, a market researcher. Online delivery is still a small slice of the $800 billion restaurant industry, but it's growing fast." [17]

■ **Reflections:**

Based on these trends, I envision multiple disruptive changes in economies across the globe in the next several decades. Impactful examples include:

- Shifts in both energy production and energy consumption will have a global impact. Several major global economic systems have depended on oil as a primary or even sole source of revenues. Continued expansion of renewable energy sources could result in a dramatic impact on revenue sources in these respective economies.

The Future of Work

- Longer term, renewable energy and battery technology innovations may in fact result in a paradigm shift for power utilities and even power grid infrastructure.

- The healthcare industry is already experiencing remarkable innovations in parallel with significant policy debates which will be largely disruptive and ideally continue to improve the quality of life for people all over the world.

- Continued impacts on brick and mortar retail storefronts driven from the on-going aggressive pioneering investments in e-commerce platforms along with transportation innovations. Consider the impact on traditional restaurants if many, if not the majority of our meals are delivered via self-driving cars or drones in the next decade or so.

- Technology has already had a rather dramatic productivity impact on farms and agriculture for several decades and will likely continue to impact the requirements for manual labor to harvest our fruits and vegetables. Additional innovations in this area are likely to trigger further disintermediation across the entire food supply chain including the introduction of self-driving trucks in the next few years, ideally helping to address world hunger across the globe.

- Consider the impact on the over 85,000 bank branches from 5,000+ financial institutions across the US [18] from the continued digitization of financial transactions in parallel with the pervasive adoption of smartphones, smart watches, and smart glasses. How many of these brick and mortar branches will still be scanning paper checks in exchange for cash in the next ten or twenty years?

- We have already witnessed remarkable changes with traditional media (i.e. television, newspapers, magazines, etc.) due to new digital media technologies and media sources. It is not too difficult to imagine that our decades old concept of network television and cable TV will disappear with the Baby

The Future of Work

Boomer generation due to the impact video streaming services. Streaming services are increasingly gaining traction with new entrants in late 2019 including Disney+ and Apple TV+. The introduction of 5G technology will accelerate this disruption. Among other things, these new media platforms have triggered fundamental shifts in the advertising sector. Current US subscriber metrics include: [19] [20] [21]

Provider	Subscribers (millions)
YouTube (users)	2,000.0
Netflix	158.8
Amazon Prime Video	96.5
Hulu	75.8
HBO NOW	23.1
Sling TV	7.0
CBS All Access	4.0

- In a matter of just a couple of years, Podcasts have arisen as a disruptive new media source. According to recent statistics, "there are more than 700,000 active podcasts and more than 29 million podcast episodes" [22] published today. Another example of a disruptive industry trend triggered by the ubiquitous presence of smartphones.

I was introduced to robotics in the manufacturing sector back in the mid-1970s. To say that a lot has changed in the past forty years' is undoubtedly an understatement. Innovations in computing infrastructure, Artificial Intelligence, Internet of Things, and robotics technologies have transformed how we think about the process of manufacturing. This massive shift in technology changes not only how we produce physical goods, but also impacts the work that is required to produce the end result.

While media attention is typically focused on Global 2000 enterprises, it is important to also recognize:

- "Firms with fewer than 500 workers accounted for 99.7 percent of those businesses. Firms with fewer than 100

The Future of Work

workers accounted for 98.2 percent. Firms with fewer than 20 workers made up 89.0 percent." [23]

- "Employer firms with fewer than 500 workers employed 46.8 percent of private sector payrolls in 2016. Employer firms with fewer than 100 workers employed 33.4 percent. Employer firms with less than 20 workers employed 16.8 percent." [24]

Another noteworthy trend is the impact that the current technology giants (i.e. Amazon, Google, Facebook, and Apple) exert on our economy and entrepreneurism today. Scott Galloway, Professor of Marketing at New York University (NYU) vehemently argues that these "monopolies" are currently stifling entrepreneurship and the ability to attract capital for traction and growth[25,26,27]. These four tech giants typically recruit and hire top graduates from the top 30 universities putting pressure on the supply of talent across the entire tech industry.

Accelerated rates of technology innovation are a leading disrupter of businesses, industry models, and ultimately jobs. Media reports echoing industry experts have issued dire warnings of the impact of AI and emerging technologies.

➔ **The Evidence:**

- "The holiday hiring frenzy is under way and robots are joining the rush to seasonal jobs. Retailers and logistics operators facing a tight labor market are ramping up automation at warehouses for the holidays, when online order volumes can surge tenfold as consumers load up digital shopping carts in the weeks around Thanksgiving and Christmas. To cope, some businesses are ordering up extra fleets of collaborative robots, or "cobots," that use cameras, lasers and sensors to navigate warehouse aisles and lead workers to the right shelves or to shuttle bins full of products between workstations." [28]
- "Robots and automation will destroy American jobs — it's a worrying refrain we hear echoed by prominent figures in academia, the private sector, and the media alike. The

The Future of Work

Brookings Institution, the management consulting firm McKinsey & Company, labor leader Andy Stern and, most recently, CNN, all have issued serious, well-researched reports and written books saying so. Silicon Valley entrepreneur and Carnegie Mellon University scholar Vivek Wadhwa goes even further, predicting that thanks to automation, unemployment will top 70% within the next century." [29]

- "[Dr.] Kai Fu Lee [CEO of Sinovation Ventures, president of the Sinovation Ventures Artificial Intelligence Institute, former President of Google China] said that he believes 40% of the world's jobs will be replaced by robots capable of automating tasks. He said that both blue collar and white collar professions will be affected, but he believes those who drive for a living could be most affected... Chauffeurs, truck drivers, anyone who does driving for a living—their jobs will be disrupted more in the 15-25 year time frame,...". [30]

- "As for jobs, Lee isn't shy about the coming disruption thanks to artificial intelligence. Customer service, telemarketing, and accounting jobs will all be subject to 'serious job displacement issues,' according to Lee, and finding new careers for workers in the field will require difficult retraining. But Lee thinks, like electricity, AI's potential to revolutionize every aspect of our daily life is more tangible than theoretical. 'AI is here to stay, and I think we need to rise up to the occasion and embrace it.'" [31]

- "...by some estimates the number of people who will lose their jobs because of robots and artificial intelligence is staggering. The McKinsey Global Institute forecasts that automation will, by 2030, destroy more than 39 million jobs in the United States, while two Oxford professors estimate that 47 percent of U.S. jobs are at risk of being automated by 2033." [32]

- "In the near future, the words tumor and heart attack will disappear from the English language. Sensors with artificial intelligence (AI) will (a) identify the genes of cancer cells circulating in our bodily fluids many years before a tumor forms, and (b) will recognize the EKG of a heart attack, locate your position, and call for an ambulance, even if you are unconscious. We will tame the two greatest killers in the U.S. today via AI. AI will also scan millions of genomes of the elderly, identify where aging takes place, and perhaps even extend the human life-span." [33]

- "Artificial intelligence (AI) and facial expression technology is being used for the first time in job interviews in the UK to identify the best candidates. Unilever, the consumer goods giant, is among companies using AI technology to analyse the language, tone and facial expressions of candidates when they are asked a set of identical job questions which they film on their mobile phone or laptop. The algorithms select the best applicants by assessing their performances in the videos against about 25,000 pieces of facial and linguistic information compiled from previous interviews of those who have gone on to prove to be good at the job." [34]

Artificial Intelligence (AI) is not a new concept. However, with a lower barrier to entry at reduced costs, new businesses have emerged that are building AI-based solutions and existing technology businesses are introducing AI into their product suites. The following chart highlights the eb and flow of AI during the past few decades.

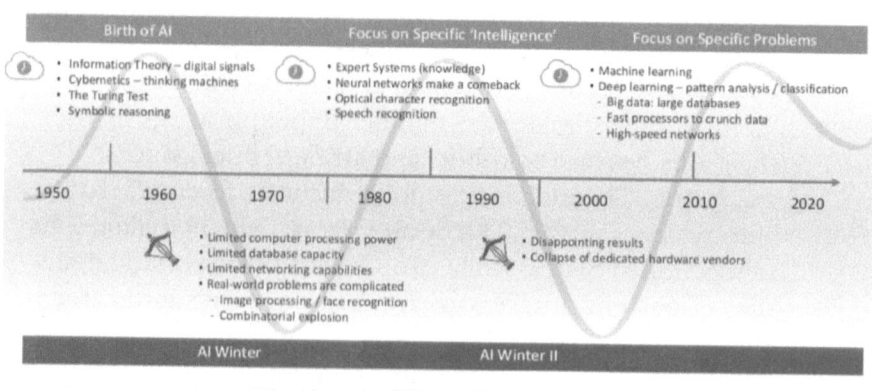

Source: harmon.ie [35]

The Future of Work

There have been numerous, sometimes rather alarming books, articles, and posts regarding the potentially dramatic impact on humans and work including historian Yuval Noah Harari that have caused me to sit back in my chair and ponder the future.

- "The automation revolution will make a lot of jobs disappear. This is not necessarily such a bad scenario. The question is whether it will be possible to support people's lives and the development of their emotional and spiritual lives without jobs. Many jobs—maybe even most jobs—that exist today are not worth defending. What we need to protect is the humans. In the current political and economic system, if you want to have your basic needs fulfilled and, for many people, to have meaning and purpose in your life, you need a job. If we could achieve these other aims without a job, then many jobs are not worth protecting. Many jobs are very difficult, very boring, very unfulfilling. People do them because they have to, not because it's really their dream to be a cashier or to drive a truck. If you can be released from these hours of working, you could perhaps develop your human potential in a much fuller way. In this sense, you are becoming more human." [36]

While media stories trigger alarmists into action, many experts argue that the ultimate impact on our economies and jobs will not be nearly as drastic. In the United States, our workforce has persevered through the Industrial Age, multiple World Wars and other military skirmishes, and multiple financial crisis over the past one hundred plus years including our most recent Great Recession. There are many voices that see light through the fog including Dr. Ichak Adizes and other researchers.

- "I believe that this is still a field of society that artificial intelligence will not be able to penetrate, at least not yet. Artificial intelligence cannot deal with emotions, cannot replace humans in the spheres of social work, community-building, and team-building. I believe the future for those disempowered by artificial intelligence lies in emotional professions. This economic sphere is already growing.

The Future of Work

Psychotherapy, family therapy, life-coaching—these professions have been growing and are the fad of today." [37]

- "'Broadly speaking, jobs that operate in non-predictable environments involving high levels of human contract and the most fundamental human attributes – especially creativity and social intelligence – are most likely to grow.' 'Ultimately, it is our policy response, rather than technological capabilities per se, that will determine the nature, speed and outcome of this structural transformation'" [38]

- "Technological advancement is one undeniable force that will shape the future of work. It is already happening: AI is entering the workplace today at a rapid clip, offloading certain tasks and displacing workers from jobs. Without deliberate effort to apply emerging technologies to promote a more inclusive and equitable work environment in 2030, the advances in technology may not yield as positive a future. With the benefit of a long view, however, we can imagine how AI in the workplace can generate a variety of new work roles and create 'new, uniquely human' jobs." [39]

To put things in perspective, compare the slope of the following curves that predict the increased impact from technological advances on our lives in the next five, twenty, and fifty years.

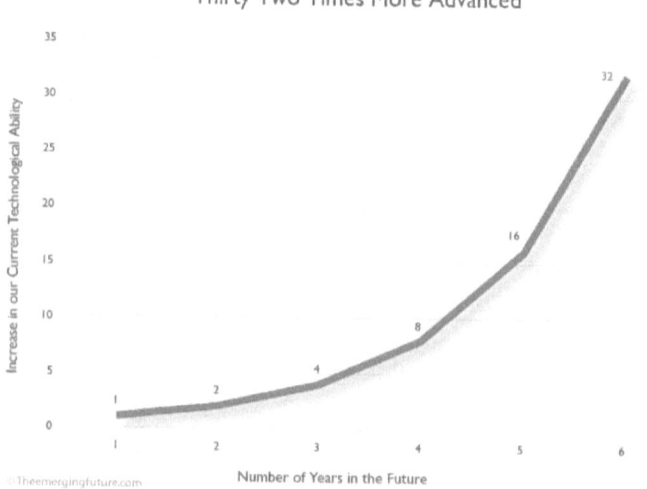

The Future of Work

Human Intuitive Perspective of Technological Advancement in Twenty Years
A Million Times More Advanced

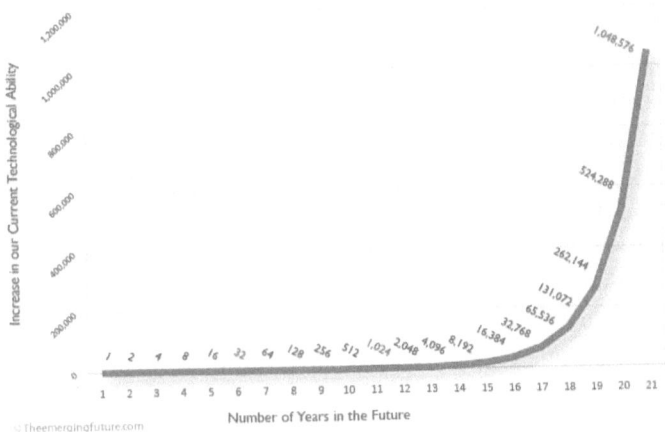

Human Intuitive Perspective of Technological Advancement in Fifty Years
A Quadrillion Times More Advanced

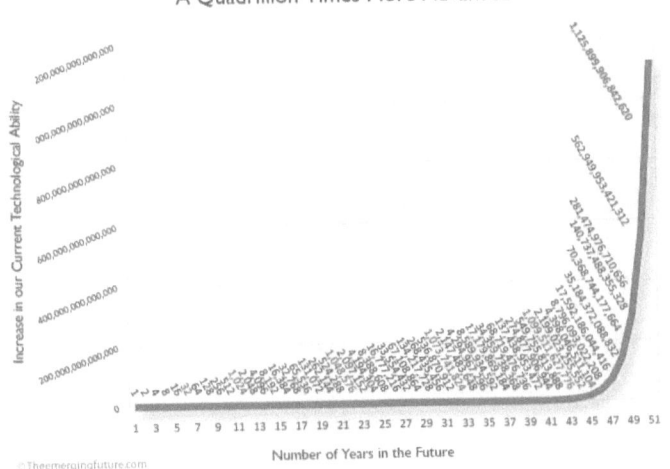

Source: The Emerging Future [40] [41] [42]

These graphs demonstrate how challenging it is to predict changes that will impact our professional and personal lives during the next five years. They also illustrate the impossible task of predicting the impact of technology advances in the next twenty years, let alone fifty years

The Future of Work

when children born today will be midway through their lives. Attempting to contemplate the changes that we will face in the next ten, twenty, and especially fifty years is literally mind-numbing.

■ **Reflections:**

- Think about the last time you had to drive to a plaza to meet with your travel agent to plan your next family vacation, or stop by AAA to pick up your TripTik Travel Planner? How about the last time you traveled to a car dealership to pick up a brochure on the latest models of your favorite car manufacturer along with features, packages, and prices? If you think about it long enough, there are more than likely dozens of professions that you depended on a decade or more ago that either no longer exist or are slowly fading away. Can you think of any additional jobs or professions that will no longer exist in 2030?

The Future of Work

DEMOGRAPHIC SHIFTS

"Each generation imagines itself to be more intelligent than the one that went before it, and wiser than the one that comes after it."

— George Orwell

Another set of relevant and fundamentally key macro trends that impact the future of work are the result of major demographic shifts. These four demographic shifts include:

1) **Baby Boomer Generation Retirements**

2) **Worker Longevity**

3) **Women's Participation in the Labor Force**

4) **Impact of new Generational Perspectives and Priorities**

I'll review each of these factors independently in the following sections.

1) Baby Boomer Generation Retirements

→ The Evidence:

- "Close to 10,000 baby boomers hit age 65 every day." [43]
- "27.1 percent of Americans were 55 or older in 2000, rising to 36.2 percent in 2018". [44]
- "Baby Boomers have always had an outsize presence compared with other generations. They peaked at 78.8 million in 1999 and have remained the largest living adult generation." [45]

The Future of Work

- "There were an estimated 74.1 million Boomers in 2016. By midcentury, the Boomer population is projected to dwindle to 16.6 million." [46]

The chart below illustrates a well-known fact that a substantial number of Baby Boomers will be leaving the workforce throughout the next decade. This trend will ultimately trigger a tremendous number of new job opportunities for younger generations to fill. While this can be viewed as a positive trend, it also includes the consequence that a tremendous wealth of institutional knowledge is walking out the door during this period. This knowledge is a critical part of every organization's intellectual property.

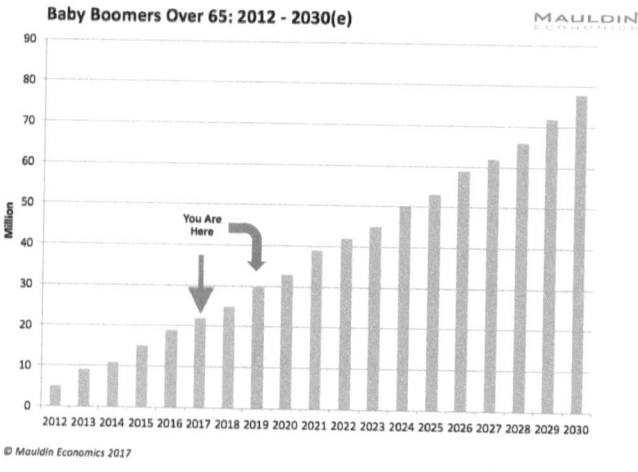

Source: Mauldin Economics [47]

It is also noteworthy that due to continuous changes in the nature of work triggered by innovation and automation, Baby Boomer retirements will not ultimately trigger a one-for-one job opportunity for a Gen Xer or Millennial workers.

2) Worker Longevity

→ The Evidence:

The Future of Work

- "There is growing awareness that increasing longevity will have major implications for how people manage their work lives and careers. Rising life expectancy means the level of savings required to provide a reasonable income for retirement at age 65 is becoming increasingly infeasible for most people. We predict that, given the average level of savings in advanced economies, many people currently in their mid-40s are likely to need to work into their early to mid-70s; many currently in their 20s (many of whom could live to be over 100) will be working into their late 70s, and even into their 80s." [48]

- "Work will not be defined by what people do, but by what people learn. For almost the past 100 years the concept of a career has been divided into four basic stages. Up to around 23 we go to school, from around 23 to 30 we choose a career path, from 30 to 65 we work in the same basic types of jobs, and after about age 65 we stop working. The assumption was people would not make major changes in the nature of their work past the age of about 30. This concept is being completely obliterated by digitalization and automation. Anyone who thinks they will be doing the same thing in 15 years that they are doing now is setting themselves up for job loss and unemployment. As more people accept the reality that no type of work is safe from automation or radical transformation, employees will expect and even demand that work enable them to learn new skills to prepare them for future jobs." [49]

- "If we can expect to live to be 100, then it will mean our work lives will stretch over 60 years! As our economy is transforming fast, new jobs will be created, many companies will die, sectors will change, new technologies will require new skills and the way we work will undergo further changes. Who could possibly plan for a 60-year career in a fast-changing environment? The only certainty is that more career transitions will be necessary both to avoid complete boredom and to get new skills when the old ones are obsolete." [50]

- "The Office for National Statistics estimates that one in three babies born in Britain today will live to 100. Some scientists think people could even live to 150. Already droves of people

are 'un-retiring' and going back to work. Advances in biology and neuroscience will help us stay younger longer." [51]
- "New ecosystems will emerge with significant sectoral changes. « There will be substantial changes in who people work for ». A century ago, the average life of an S&P 500 company was 67 years. By 2013, it had reduced to 15 years. In other words, people live longer but companies die sooner (not that the two things are necessarily related)." [52]
- "Basically, we have discovered that aging is more malleable than we thought, we are living longer and have more time and need to reshape our lives accordingly. That has enormous implications for us as individuals and our relationships, for firms both in terms of workers and consumers; and offers opportunities for new products with outstanding value. It also creates an extensive government agenda." [53]
- "To retire at 65, millennials will need to save nearly half of their paycheck" [54]

In their book, "The 100-Year Life – Living and Working in an Age of Longevity" [55], Lynda Gratton and Andrew Scott argue that we are at the early stages of a transition from a three-stage to a multiple-stage life. In other words, many of us from the Baby Boomer generation have lived in a "three-stage life" paradigm with the expectations that we would invest:

Stage 1: Roughly 20 years in education and training to prepare for;

Stage 2: A potentially 40 – 45 year professional career, ideally with the same company or institution, and most certainly in the same profession, then hopefully;

Stage 3: Another 20 or more years enjoying the fruits of their labors in retirement.

According to their research, children born in the West today have a 50 percent chance of living more than 105 years. If we can expect to live to be 100 or more, then it will mean our work lives will potentially stretch several decades to over 60 years or more. I found the following illustration to be quite intriguing and enlightening the first time I came across it.

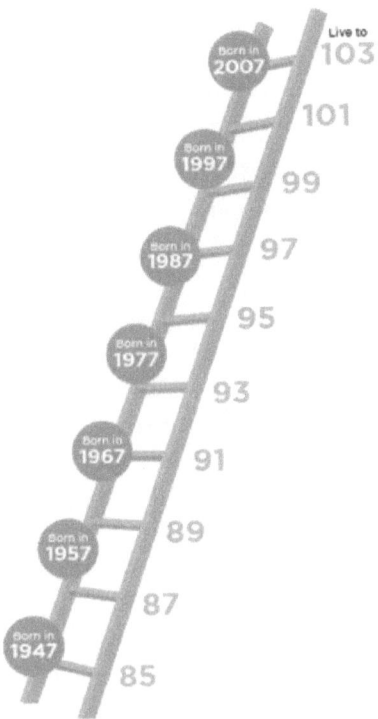

Source: The 100-Year Life [56]

In this context, retiring at 65 years old and living another 40 plus years on a pension, retirement savings, or just Social Security will not be feasible for many people. While many institutions will feel the impact of Baby Boomer retirements today, longer term they may also benefit from access to a workforce that could be available for productive work several decades longer than previous generations.

3) Women's Participation in the Workforce

→ **The Evidence:**

- "The proportion of women with college degrees in the labor force has almost quadrupled since 1970. More than 40

percent of women in the labor force had college degrees in 2016, compared with 11 percent in 1970." [57]
- "Women's participation in the U.S. labor force has climbed since WWII: from 32.7 percent in 1948 to 56.8 percent in 2016." [58]
- "The birth rate in the U.S. has dropped dramatically over the last 10 years. The U.S. has reached an all-time low of 60.2 births per 1,000 women of child-bearing age." [59]
- "In an experiment, researchers found that investors were more likely to bet that a company's stock price would increase if it had more women on staff than average. That suggests investors see value in gender diversity and that companies that hire more women could see their stock prices rise." [60]
- "From 2010 to 2017, Letcher County saw a greater shift in the gender balance of its labor force than almost any other county in the United States. The share of women in the work force rose substantially in places throughout Central Appalachia, as well as in parts of the industrial Midwest and the rural South. But few places have seen a more dramatic change than Letcher County, in hilly Eastern Kentucky, where for generations the archetypal worker was a brawny, coal-dusted man in reflective overalls. Just 10 years ago, nearly three-fifths of the work force was male. Now the majority is female." [61]
- "A growing body of research links greater gender diversity on teams and in corporate management to more innovation and better financial performance. That business case is a big reason more senior leaders at companies—73%—say achieving equality for women in the workplace is a priority, up from 56% four years ago." [62]
- "More women are becoming senior leaders. This is driven by two trends. First, more women are being hired at the director level and above than in past years. Second, senior-level women are being promoted on average at a higher rate than men." [63]
- "Today, 44 percent of companies have three or more women in their C-suite, up from 29 percent of companies in 2015." [64]

The Future of Work

- "With more than three months to go, 2019 is already turning out to be an inspirational year for women entrepreneurs working toward closing the gender gap in VC. As of the end of August, companies founded solely by women have garnered around $2.4 billion of VC [Venture Capital] dollars in the US in 2019, on pace to surpass last year's decade-high of $3 billion." [65]

Women's voices are increasingly being heard as we witness rising numbers of women in key public sector roles, corporate boardrooms, and strategic roles in the workplace. The differences between women and men is also gaining additional visibility as evidenced from increased research and publications including "Invisible Women: Data Bias in a World Designed for Men" (2019) by writer, broadcaster, and feminist activist Caroline Criado Perez [66] [67]. The evolution of the workplace will continue to shift as women increasingly play key leadership roles and have considerably more influence over policies, company values, cultures, and strategies.

Another trend that will continue to influence the workplace is an increase in the percentage of minorities entering the workforce, led predominantly by women.

- "The surge of minority women getting jobs has helped push the U.S. workforce across a historic threshold. For the first time, most new hires of prime working age (25 to 54) are people of color, according to a Washington Post analysis of data the Labor Department began collecting in the 1970s. Minority hires overtook white hires last year. Women are predominantly driving this trend, which is so powerful that even many women who weren't thinking about working — because they were in school, caring for kids or at home for other reasons — are being lured into employment, according to The Post's analysis." [68]

The Future of Work

In a first, most new prime-age workers are minorities

What new prime-age (25 through 54) workers were doing a month ago; shown as 24-month average relative to a group's share of the labor force

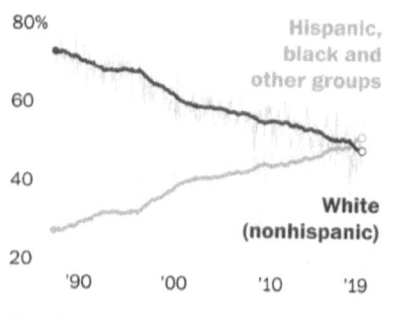
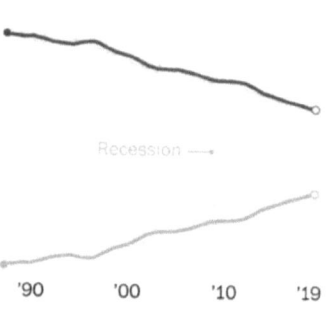

Note: Race includes Hispanic background.
Source: Labor Department via IPUMS with guidance from Nick Bunker at Indeed, Ernie Tedeschi at Evercore ISI and Marianne Wanamaker at University of Tennessee Knoxville.
THE WASHINGTON POST

Source: The Washington Post [69]

Additional evidence of the considerable changes that are underway in the makeup of our workforce at this time include:

- "While the job market has rebounded nicely since the Great Recession, one segment of the population hasn't shared in the recovery. Men between the ages of 25 and 54 are still less likely to be working than they once were, says Melissa Kearney, an economics professor at the University of Maryland. In 1968, about 95% of men in their prime working years held jobs. The number has fallen to just 86%, even though today's job market is ultra-tight. Kearney says the recovery and employment growth in the past five years are very encouraging. But, she says, 'I still see a lot of data that suggests we have structural challenges, and we need to be doing more to try and draw more prime-age workers back into the workforce.'" [70]
- "... the unemployment rate is a very low 3.8%. But a lot of men don't show up in the government's numbers because they aren't looking for work anymore..." [71]

The Future of Work

4) ## Impact of new Generational Perspectives and Priorities

→ **The Evidence:**

- "Millennials are expected to overtake Boomers in population in 2019 as their numbers swell to 73 million and Boomers decline to 72 million. Generation X (ages 36 to 51 in 2016) is projected to pass the Boomers in population by 2028." [72]
- "Generation Z has arrived. Sixty-one million strong in the U.S. alone, they will comprise 30% of the workforce by 2030. They are more diverse, more educated, and more technologically adept than any previous generation." [73]
- "Gen Zs are Anxious, Entrepreneurial and Determined to Avoid Their Predecessor's Mistakes. The wild card for employers is to what extent Gen Zs will take an entrepreneurial path rather than a corporate one. Big corporations, which have few qualms about "downsizing" employees when it suits them, are no longer assumed to be the stable alternative." [74]
- "Just over half of post-Millennial is non-white, making them the most diverse generation in the history of the United Sates. And at 61 million strong, they are a larger cohort than either Baby Boomers or Millennials." [75]

The following charts provide additional insights into demographic changes that will impact the workforce over the next several decades.

The Future of Work

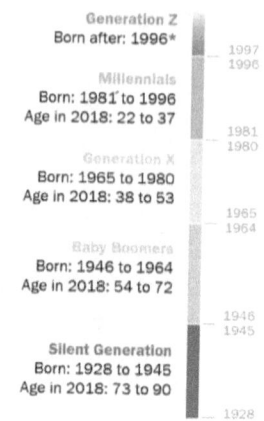

Source: Pew Research Center [76]

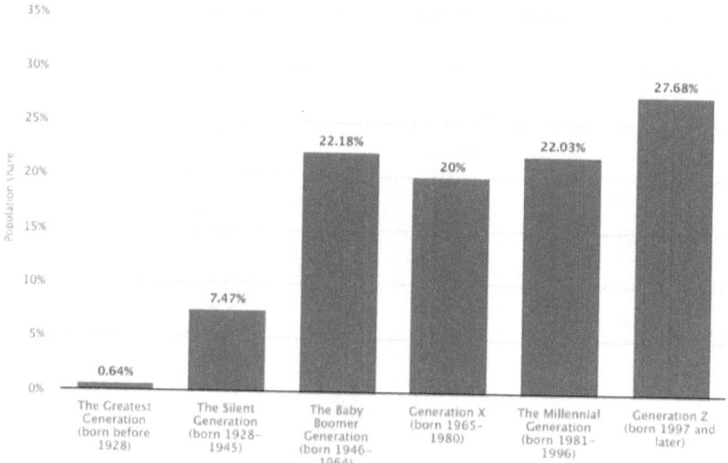

Source: Statista [77]

The Future of Work

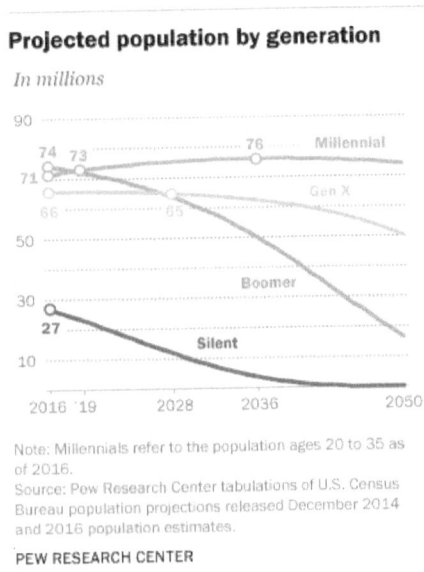

Source: Pew Research Center [78]

2019 was a pivotal year when the number of Millennials surpassed the Baby Boomers in the United States. The delta between the two generations will accelerate quickly over the next decade and beyond. Much of the research for this book has been focused on contemplating the state of work for the Generation Alpha workforce which have and will continue to interact with technology at a very young age.

- "By 2025, which is the year when the youngest Alphas are born, Generation Alpha will account to 2 billion of the global population. Generation Alpha is considered to be the most technological-infused demographic up to date. Generation Alpha are children born from 2010 to 2025. They are the first generation entirely born within the 21st century. They are also known as the iGeneration. They are the children of the Millennials. Generation Alpha use smartphones and tablets naturally. These children were born along with iPhones, iPads, and applications. They don't know or can imagine how life was without them. They are not afraid of technology or touching buttons to learn what those buttons do. Alphas learn by doing. Generation Alpha is growing up with the

The Future of Work

familiar voice of Siri, Alexa, and Google Assistant in their home. In the world of the Alphas, interacting with Artificial Intelligence and voice assistants is simply natural." [79]

■ **Reflections:**

- Attempting to digest and comprehend the number of workforce changes underway is overwhelming. I envision these concurrent changes this will introduce many new challenges to Human Resource (People) professionals and all professionals in leadership roles.

- On a positive note, the trends underway noted in this chapter will also provide ample opportunities for businesses and institutions to differentiate themselves in how they proactively respond to workforce trends.

- In the decades ahead, if people are continuing to work well into their 80s, 90s, or even 100s – will sabbaticals, or extended leaves from work every five or ten years, become a common practice in the majority of workplaces?

These generational transitions will impact the workplace as corporate and institutional leadership passes to new generations. We are witnessing the introduction of a new wave of workplace leadership as increasing numbers of women, minorities, Millennials, and Gen Z professionals continue to represent a great proportion of the workforce.

The Future of Work

ALWAYS-ON, ALWAYS-CONNECTED WORLD

"The thrill of victory in business blows away the thrill of victory in sports. Business is a sport 24/7/365."

— *Mark Cuban*

The acceleration of advancements in mobile, wearable technologies, and sensors everywhere combined with the pervasiveness of social media and collaboration platforms have far reaching and potentially remarkable impact on our daily lives. This combination of these technologies has spawned a 24 by 7 by 365 "always-on" world. Geographic boundaries have been digitally collapsed along with the need for common physical workspaces for communication and collaboration.

The concept of a standard structured workday has shifted to align with this new always-on dynamic. Deployment of 5G technology infrastructure that begun in 2019 will further fuel and accelerate this trend. With a theoretical top speed of 100 Gbps, 5G technology is an order of magnitude faster than 4G. Connecting to cloud computing resources at these speeds means that 5G network infrastructure will lead to:

- Vast increase in the amount of data captured in the cloud

- Real-time monitoring of virtually everything powered by an explosion of Internet of Things (IoT) technologies

- Continued proliferation of real-time digital video

→ **The Evidence:**

- "After years of hype about gigabit speeds that will let you download full-length movies in mere seconds, 5G is a reality. All four wireless carriers have flipped the switch on 5G in the

The Future of Work

U.S., and you can buy 5G phones that can take advantage of faster speeds on those networks." [80]
- "… the industry of wearable devices has slowly and quietly grown into a major market force in the last few years. From a total of 27.4 million devices shipped in 2015, more than 178 million wearable devices were purchased in 2018. For 2019, the industry is on track for a 25.8% increase in sales volume, which corresponds to about 255 million units. In terms of value, the volume of wearable devices expected to be sold in 2019 could amount to about $42 billion." [81]
- "The Internet of Things is one of the most defining technologies of the Fourth Industrial Revolution. It can transform how organizations design, produce and sell their products and services, as well as how they become part of a larger ecosystem – both physical and digital." [82]
- "SpaceX, the private spaceflight company known for reusable rockets and a giant, shiny Starship, will begin offering its own satellite internet service in 2020… The initial Starlink plan called for a megaconstellation of 12,000 satellites, and SpaceX recently filed paperwork with the International Telecommunication Union (ITU) to launch another 30,000 satellites." [83]

This shift in network speed and capacity translates into new job and career opportunities, many of which do not exist at this time. Innovative wearable technologies will spawn new career opportunities and ultimately impact an array of industries including healthcare, transportation, media and entertainment, security, ecommerce, manufacturing, energy, agriculture, financial services, education, and real estate sectors to name a few. [84]

Beyond connecting people, social media and collaboration platforms are pervasive across the globe, affecting when, where, and how we work. 5G network infrastructure increases the real-time and always-on nature of these platforms, seamlessly bridging geographic boundaries. The next generation of "digital natives" are a major force in the new workplace as mobile devices and network capacity reduce barriers create and access digital content.

The Future of Work

→ **The Evidence:**

- "YouTube, Instagram and Snapchat are the most popular online platforms among U.S. teens. Fully 95% of teens have access to a smartphone, and 45% say they are online 'almost constantly'". [85]
- "Now, in 2019, users are watching 4,333,560 [YouTube] videos every minute. 300 hours of video are uploaded to YouTube every minute!" [86]
- "Instagram users upload over 100 million photos and videos every day. That is 69,444 million posts every minute!" [87]

While there are numerous benefits from these technological advancements, I also fear that there are serious consequences that we will have to address or at least acknowledge.

- "More than a third of millennials and Gen Z (36%) say they spend two hours or more checking their smartphones during the workday. That adds up to at least 10 hours every week when they're doing something outside their job responsibilities. This behavior isn't limited to junior workers either; overall, just under two-thirds of survey respondents (62%) spend about an hour per day looking at their phones." [88]

■ **Reflections:**

- I predict that 5G will emerge as a truly revolutionary innovation in wireless networking technology and will likely be more disruptive than the introduction of the iPod and the iPhone in the last two decades.

- While I have been a technology enthusiast throughout my entire professional career, I am concerned that yet more always-on, always-connected related advancements will result in additional continuous distractions and challenge our limited attention spans even further. The end result is that they will likely ultimately continue to be a detriment and threat to productivity in the workplace.

The Future of Work

- Will the combination of the continued miniaturization of hardware devices and ubiquitous high-speed connectivity everywhere on all things challenge our current paradigms of offices, conference rooms, desks, etc.? Consider the aggregate impact on productivity if workers gained 54 minutes per day, five days per week (225 hours per year) if commute time was eliminated for a high percentage of workers? [89]

Our emerging always-on, always-connected anywhere and everywhere world where mobile devices and sensors on everything will soon be ubiquitous throughout the planet. It is difficult for me to envision and predict what we will be carrying and wearing a decade from now. Regardless, this trend will have a significant impact on jobs and careers along with our daily personal lives.

The Future of Work

REINVENTION OF HIGHER EDUCATION

"Knowledge is power. Information is liberating. Education is the premise of progress, in every society, in every family."

– Kofi Annan

I anticipate that major transformations will be underway within our institutions of education and learning in the coming decades. I believe that the standard curriculum for core sciences, social sciences, and liberal arts education will most likely continue into the foreseeable future. Over time, the impact from the major paradigm shifts relative to jobs and careers underway will especially challenge higher education institutions to reinvent themselves in order to continue to be relevant to the increasingly rapidly changing workforce requirements. I predict that this trend will also have a substantial impact on how employers continue to promote and foster an environment of lifelong learning and continuous training within their workplace.

Our Higher Education systems are currently being disrupted and reinvented to meet the new employment paradigm. The pace of change and impact of technological innovations is challenging traditional academic paradigms during a time when higher education institutions are continuing to deal with the transition from textbooks to digital media, Massive Open Online Courses (MOOCs), and online universities for instruction. The jobs in the coming decades will also demand continuous learning instead of, or over-and-above, traditional baccalaureate and master's degrees. The following report and analysis from The Manhattan Institute, "Six Forces Disrupting Higher Education,"[90] caught my attention recently. In summary, they reported on the following trends:

1. Starting in 2025, the number of college bound students is likely to decline substantially

2. Tuition is soaring at rates far higher than inflation

The Future of Work

3. Student loan debt is soaring

4. The over-education problem

5. University inequality

6. MOOCs [Massive Open Online Courses]

→ **The Evidence:**

- "Today's students must be prepared for jobs that don't exist yet, but also for jobs that exist now but will look drastically different." [91]
- "The greatest threat to workers today is not a robot, but another worker who knows how to work with robots and other technology – a worker who is adaptable and possesses the very human skills of communication, complex problem solving, and self-management." [92]
- "The fact is, the workplace today, and in the future, requires creativity, not repetitive task completion – technology can handle that. There are estimates that as much as 50% of all jobs could be automated in the next decade or two. Yet, while there is good reason to believe that relative few jobs will be completely automated in the immediate future, some jobs will change. The key issue is how 'routine' the work is. It's not a high- versus low-wage or high- versus low-skill story, but rather, which parts of a job can be automated." [93]
- "Five years from now, over one-third of skills (35%) that are considered important in today's workforce will have changed. By 2020, the Fourth Industrial Revolution will have brought us advanced robotics and autonomous transport, artificial intelligence and machine learning, advanced materials, biotechnology and genomics. These developments will transform the way we live, and the way we work. Some jobs will disappear, others will grow and jobs that don't even exist today will become commonplace. What is certain is that the future workforce will need to align its skillset to keep pace." [94]
- "I suggest a revolution in education is needed. We must be taught not to know, but how to learn. We must nourish

The Future of Work

people with the passion to continually learn from everything they encounter in life—not just from textbooks. We should teach people to be open-minded and not to be ashamed to claim ignorance, thus encouraging a greater willingness to learn more and more." [95]

- "...the attraction of a Duke Daytime MBA appears to have slid. Applications have declined 20% in the last three years, mirroring a similar slide at many business schools." [96]

- "Yet the economy of 2007 is a low bar for economic opportunity. Relative to the full employment economy of the late 1990s and 2000, the shares of young graduates who are unemployed and underemployed, and generally 'idled' by the economy (neither working nor in school), are still quite high." [97]

- "When businesses don't get what they need from the new college graduates they hire, one of their first punching bags is the college system itself. 'The future of work is arriving faster than the speed of light,' said Sue Bhatia, founder of Rose International, a staffing agency based in Chesterfield, Mo. 'The educational models of memory-based knowledge accumulation that we rely on are outmoded and will not sufficiently prepare young people for solid careers. We're living in an era of a lag between the old model of college education and the coming future of work. Unfortunately, our young professionals are educated for a world that will not exist as it currently does.'" [98]

- "In fall 2019, overall postsecondary enrollments decreased 1.3 percent or more than 231,000 students from the previous fall to 17.9 million students. For the first time in the decade, the nation's fall unduplicated enrollments fell below 18 million students and declined by more than 2 million students." [99]

- "The foreign undergraduate head count in U.S. colleges and universities fell about 2 percent in the last school year, the first annual decline on that measure in more than a decade, according to a study. The report from the Institute of International Education, funded by the State Department and made public Monday, suggests challenges for the United States as it seeks to maintain dominance in global higher education. International undergraduates in U.S. schools totaled about 431,900 in the 2018-2019 academic year, down more than 10,000. That ended 12 straight years of growth of a crucial source of tuition revenue for colleges and universities. International students pay higher out-of-state rates at public universities and tend to receive far less financial aid than domestic students. They also contribute to the education of U.S. students, educators say, by helping to create a more diverse and cosmopolitan campus climate." [100]

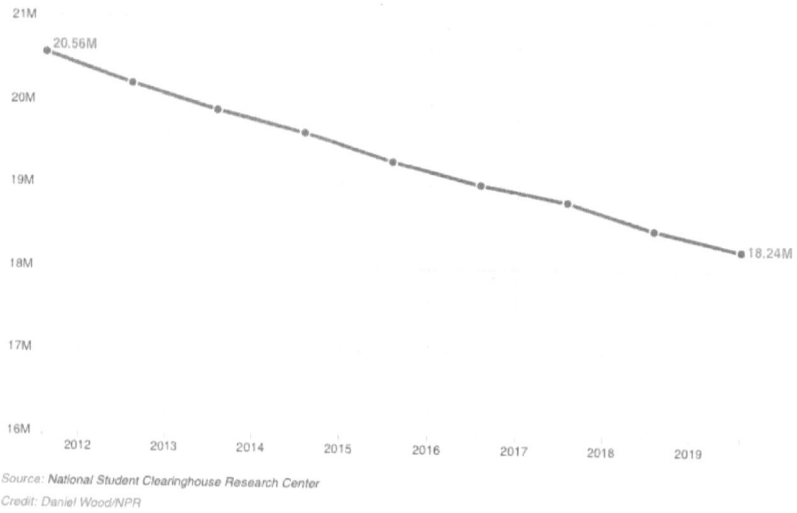

Student Enrollment At U.S. Colleges Down 11% Since 2011
About 2.3 million fewer students enrolled in college this fall than in fall 2011.

Source: National Student Clearinghouse Research Center
Credit: Daniel Wood/NPR

Source: National Student Clearinghouse Research Center [101]

In respect to trends for tuition fees and the cost of education in general, the United States Bureau of Labor Statistics (BLS) published the following chart which indicated an increase of over 150% in college tuition fees in the two decades between 1997 and 2017.

The Future of Work

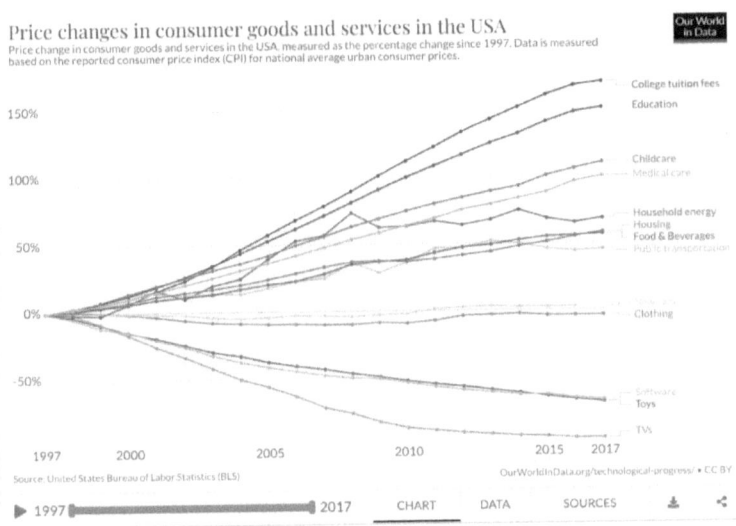

Source: Our World in Data [102]

I discovered two somewhat surprising and nonintuitive opposing trends in the charts below.

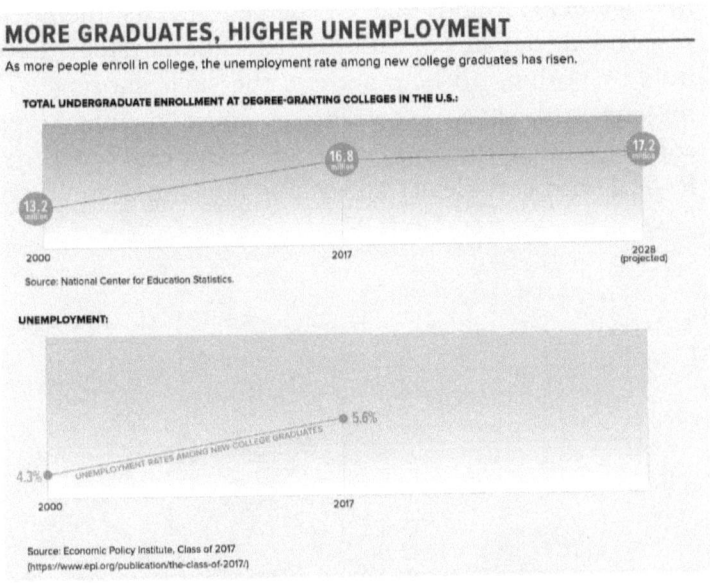

Source: National Center for Education Statistics and Economic Policy Institute [103]

The Future of Work

In the years ahead, "soft skills" (the personal attributes, personality traits, inherent social cues, and communication abilities needed for success on the job. Soft skills characterize how a person interacts in his or her relationships with others [104]) will increasingly be valued and essential over traditional "hard skills" (part of the skill set that is required for a job. They include the expertise necessary for an individual to successfully do the job. They are job-specific and are typically listed in job postings and job descriptions. Hard skills are acquired through formal education and training programs, including college, apprenticeships, short-term training classes, online courses, certification programs, as well as by on-the-job training [105]) as evidenced by the research and analysis from multiple industry experts and noted in the following table.

Unfortunately, it appears that our current educational institutions have not been successful in addressing this opportunity. For instance, a recent published report by SHRM identified:

- "In a 2019 report, the Society for Human Resource Management found that 51 percent of its members who responded to a survey said that education systems have done little or nothing to help address the skills shortage. The top missing soft skills, according to these members: problem solving, critical thinking, innovation and creativity; the ability to deal with complexity and ambiguity; and communication." [106]

The Future of Work

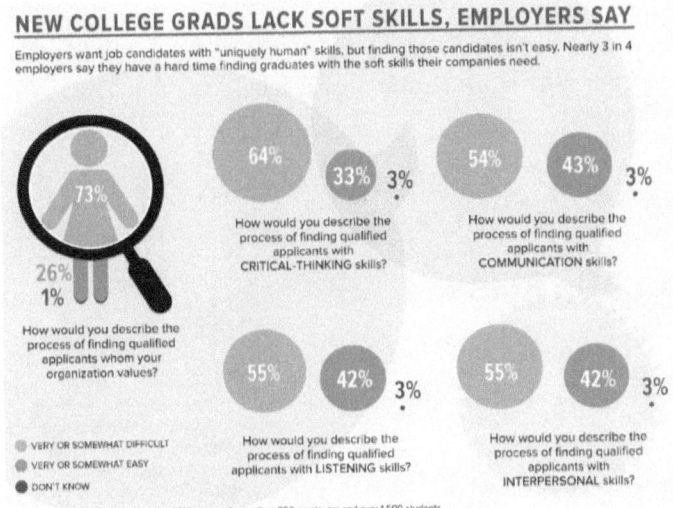

Source: SHRM / Cengage/Morning Consult [107]

The recent Cengage survey noted that "The top skills today's employers are looking for in candidates include:" [108]

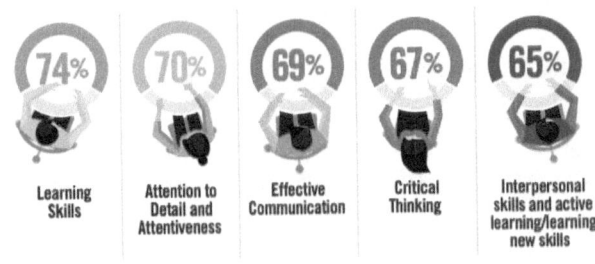

Source: Cengage [109]

The Future of Work

A recent report from the World Economic Forum also highlighted the critical need for soft skills in the workplace.

Top 10 skills

in 2020	in 2015
1. Complex Problem Solving	1. Complex Problem Solving
2. Critical Thinking	2. Coordinating with Others
3. Creativity	3. People Management
4. People Management	4. Critical Thinking
5. Coordinating with Others	5. Negotiation
6. Emotional Intelligence	6. Quality Control
7. Judgment and Decision Making	7. Service Orientation
8. Service Orientation	8. Judgment and Decision Making
9. Negotiation	9. Active Listening
10. Cognitive Flexibility	10. Creativity

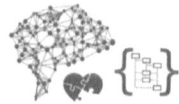 

Source: Future of Jobs Report, World Economic Forum

Source: World Economic Forum [110]

- "Despite a report by the World Economic Forum in 2018 suggesting robot automation will create more jobs than they displace, you'll still do well to keep on top of your creativity skills and maintain an innovative mindset. Much like having an excellent sense of social intelligence, natural creativity is something which can't be easily replicated by the latest digital technologies. As long as you can think outside the box, you'll be just fine." [111]

TopUniversities.com (Quacquarelli Symonds Limited) with the help of the University of the Witwatersrand identified five skills that job seekers will need to succeed in a future career: [112]

The Future of Work

1. Cognitive flexibility

2. Digital literacy and computational thinking

3. Judgement and decision-making

4. Emotional and social intelligence

5. Creative and innovative mindset

- "Of course, humanities students should not abandon their love for the arts, as key to a student's future success and happiness is the pursuit of a career they enjoy. In fact, five of the key skills for future employment involve the use of key human skills such as": [113]

    1. Mental Elasticity and Complex Problem Solving

    2. Critical Thinking

    3. Creativity

    4. People Skills

    5. Interdisciplinary Knowledge

Studies by Harvard Business School and other organizations highlight the risks of maintaining expectations that all jobs should require a four-year degree:

- "Degree inflation—the rising demand for a four-year college degree for jobs that previously did not require one—is a substantive and widespread phenomenon that is making the U.S. labor market more inefficient. Postings for many jobs traditionally viewed as middleskills jobs (those that require employees with more than a high school diploma but less than a college degree) in the United States now stipulate a college degree as a minimum education requirement, while

only a third of the adult population possesses this credential."
114

- "The survey also reveals that many employers find middle-skills workers with relevant experience equally or more productive than college graduates. Employers also report that hiring college graduates makes middle-skills jobs harder to fill and results in higher turnover and less engaged employees. In addition to the survey, Dismissed by Degrees draws on an analysis of 26 million job postings to dissect the degree gap across occupations. The analysis shows that if the current pace of degree inflation continues, 6.2 million more middle-skills jobs will be at risk as they shift to a four-year college degree requirement." 115

- "Degree inflation hurts the average American's ability to enter and stay in the workforce. Many middle-skills jobs synonymous with middle-class lifestyles and upward mobility—such as supervisors, support specialists, sales representatives, inspectors and testers, clerks, and secretaries and administrative assistants—are now considered hard-to-fill jobs because employers prefer candidates who are college graduates. Even workers who have relevant experience are excluded from consideration by automated tools that weed out candidates who do not have a college degree. In our survey, two-thirds of companies acknowledge that stipulating a four-year degree excludes qualified candidates from consideration." 116

While the analysis above suggests that college degrees may not be required for many jobs and professions, there is also considerable evidence that adults that have not earned a higher education degree will be at a higher risk of maintaining employment in the decades ahead.

- "About two-thirds of workers in the U.S. don't have a college degree, which puts them at higher risk of losing work to new technologies. The researchers found that workers who didn't go to college or didn't finish high school are four times as likely to lose jobs because of automation. 'Automation could

The Future of Work

widen existing educational, income, and wealth disparities,' the economists wrote." [117]

▪ Reflections:

- Are we educating and training students that represent our future workforce today to proactively adapt to change and continuous technology innovation at an ever increasing rate?

- At what stage (i.e. elementary school, middle school, high school, and/or college or university) should we start to emphasize and concentrate on the importance of soft skills?

- Should the topic of teaching skills on the topic of proactively anticipating and responding to change along with building resiliency be incorporated into the curriculum in secondary schools?

- Will the overall impact of the trends highlighted throughout this book produce more or fewer academic positions from pK-12 through higher education institutions?

- I anticipate that some readers may not agree to many of my statements and predictions in this section, particularly education and academic professionals. Historically, much like our public sectors – academia in general can be rather slow to adapt to important trends underway. In many respects, they have been insulated from various events and trends that at times dramatically impact commercial businesses.

Bottom line is that I believe there is increasing evidence for a major paradigm shift for education and academic institutions. My current projection is that employers will be forced to play a considerably more proactive role in the on-going education and training for all of their employees to remain competitive in their respective markets.

The Future of Work

The Future of Work

GENERATIONAL EXPECTATIONS

"Corporate culture is the only sustainable competitive advantage that is completely within the control of the entrepreneur."

— *David Cummings, Co-Founder of Pardot*

I have had the satisfaction to personally experience a very diverse and inspiring professional career that has spanned five decades. My professional experience has included key leadership roles in large Fortune 500 companies, working in academia and the public sector, and over two decades working in very innovative entrepreneurial business ventures. One topic that I have focused on more recently is observing the remarkable differences across the generational perspectives in the workplace. I have observed and learned a tremendous amount from my younger colleagues, including many behaviors that I wish I had personally factored into my own personal philosophy and practice about work and work-life balance early in my career.

One key and obvious generational differences between Baby Boomers like myself and Digital Natives is how intuitive and adaptable our younger generations are with embracing technology in the workplace and their ability to adapt to the continuous evolution and introduction of new technology. There are also more subtle but very important evolutionary trends regarding the workplace itself. While I can recall dropping a dime or quarter into an empty coffee can for a community cup of coffee at work, now many institutions have fully stocked kitchens with espresso machines and in some cases on-site chefs, craft beer taps, and regularly scheduled Happy Hours – along with game tables and lots of other interesting recreational activities.

There is also a considerable difference in the design and ergonomics of office spaces. Today, many businesses have designed open office spaces to increase communication and collaboration and the feeling of community amongst their employees versus vast seas of cubicles that I remember from decades ago. While I can recall punching a

The Future of Work

timekeeping clock or entering start and stop times in a timekeeping or payroll system – today, and fortunately, there is considerably greater emphasis on delivering results versus the number of hours sitting chained to a desk.

Many businesses also permit working full or part-time remotely from a home office, co-working site, or coffee shop versus arriving in an office and sitting in a cubicle or desk next to your manager or supervisor. The following graph highlights the growth in coworking spaces in the United States from 2015 to 2022.

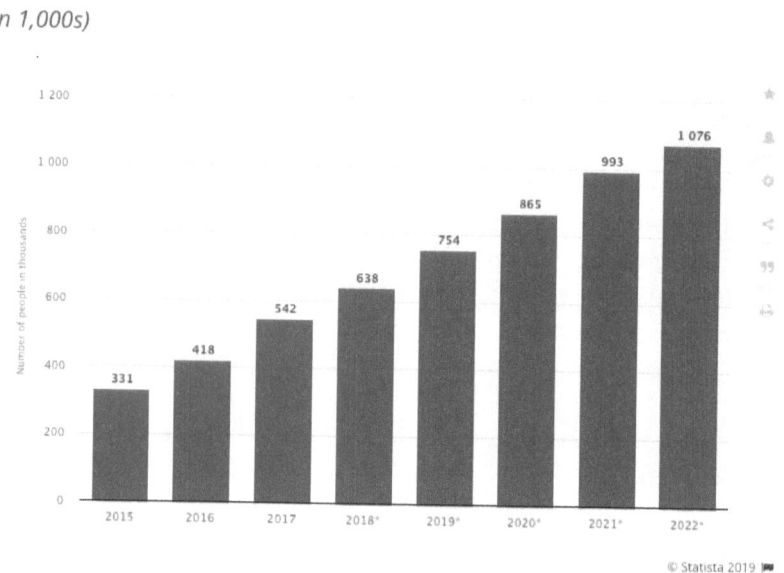

Source: Statista 2019 [118]

Companies and academic researchers have been studying productivity since Frederick W. Taylor published "The Principles of Scientific Management" [119] back in 1909. Corporations have continued to challenge their leaders and employees to continuously improve worker productivity each and every year. I found the following conclusions from a recent report published by Korn Ferry International quite interesting:

➔ **The Evidence:**

The Future of Work

- "For two months, a financial services firm cut its workweek to four eight-hour days but paid for five days—and invited university researchers to study the impact on performance. Very quickly, the results became clear: workers showed up on time and creativity burgeoned. Productivity rose 20 percent. The policy became permanent." [120]
- "In 2016, a team of researchers from Australia and Japan studied the impacts of shorter versus longer workweeks on the cognitive function of more than 6,000 men and women. They found a 25-hour workweek led to peak performance. Putting in more than 55 hours a week and not working at all were most detrimental to cognitive ability." [121]
- "Workers at Microsoft Japan enjoyed an enviable perk this summer: working four days a week, enjoying a three-day weekend — and getting their normal, five-day paycheck. The result, the company says, was a productivity boost of 40%. Microsoft Japan says it became more efficient in several areas, including lower electricity costs, which fell by 23%." [122]
- "Ireland has joined an international campaign, which aims to introduce a four-day working week. The initiative, which has been launched by 4 Day Week Ireland, aims to remove the extra day from the Irish working week in a bid to see a wide variety of different benefits. The campaign has brought together a coalition of trade unions, businesses and representative groups." [123]
- "Still, numerous studies have suggested that knowledge workers—those who rely primarily on cognitive capacity—are really only productive for about three hours a day. As time stacks up, output plummets and errors multiply." [124]
- "If performance isn't incentive enough, flexible scheduling is an increasingly valuable negotiating chip. In fact, says Vanderkam, 'younger workers view flexibility as the opening bid.' That's hardly anything for companies trying to retain talent in an age of record low unemployment to ignore, says Evelyn Orr, chief operating officer of the Korn Ferry Institute. Forcing employees to work at set times on set days could ultimately hurt the bottom line. 'The limiting factor for growth is talent,' she says." [125]

The Future of Work

■ **Reflections:**

- I have had the opportunity to hire, lead, support, and mentor well over one hundred individuals during the past decade alone. The majority of these new hires have been women and men in their 20s and early 30s. It has been fascinating to me to observe how this generation of professionals' view work, careers, and the workplace compared to my personal professional journey early in my career. I do not care to judge whether the attitudes are better or worse, but I have found that the mindsets are definitely different.

- Organization cultures are becoming increasingly transparent. In other words, what is printed on a plaque on an employee's desk, the office kitchen area, an institution's website, or LinkedIn is insignificant relative to the information that is posted on Glassdoor and various social media platforms. It is virtually impossible for a company to hide behind a set of slogans or the media published by a PR or Marketing team.

- As the rate of change in our personal and professional lives continues to accelerate, will generational differences become increasingly amplified or potentially disappear over time?

- Millions of books and articles have been published debating and discussing management and leadership techniques over the past one hundred years. What will be the potential impact on these important topics after the Baby Boomers have retired and have all been replaced by Digital Natives?

- The notion of a 9 to 5 workday and five-day workweek for information workers has puzzled me for decades. For the past 30 years, my office has been wherever my laptop happened to be located on any particular day or hour regardless of my physical location and time zone. While I'm certainly not advocating a seven-day, 16 hour work week, I continue to get frustrated when leaders become more focused on when employees arrive and depart in the office each day versus the results delivered by each employee. I envision that

The Future of Work

this model will disappear with the retirement of the Baby Boomers in leadership roles.

In summary, I believe that in order for many companies to stay competitive from a talent acquisition perspective – especially in strong economic times – Human Resource (or Human Capital Management, People, Talent, etc.) organizations and recruiting professionals must be keenly mindful about the expectations of the overall work environment, and increasingly thoughtful of the differences in expectations from the young professionals that are entering their workforce today and in the years ahead.

The Future of Work

The Future of Work

GLOBAL ECONOMIC CYCLES AND TRENDS

"As sure as the spring will follow the winter, prosperity and economic growth will follow recession."

— Bo Bennett

"The gig economy is empowerment. This new business paradigm empowers individuals to better shape their own destiny and leverage their existing assets to their benefit."

— John McAfee

Having majored in economics for my undergraduate degree, I still have a fundamental understanding of the economic concept of supply and demand, which certainly plays a role in many things including jobs and careers. I have also participated in more economic cycles that I care to remember, especially the downturns. I have had the distinct pleasure of participating in major hiring sprees of dozens and even hundreds of new employees at a frenetic pace in a short period of time. Sadly, I have also been required to participate in the decision-making process of far too many layoffs, including one business that executed a series of layoffs that impacted thousands of employees and their families over a period of several years. I can't think of a more challenging and difficult experience as a manager than the responsibility of dismissing or laying off a member of your staff.

In other words, supply and demand applies to employers and the workers along the lines of:

- When there is a high volume of open jobs, it typically results in a lower number of available candidates. This provides an obvious advantage to candidate. Employers are required to be more creative, strategic, and competitive on how they attract and retain quality candidates – including higher wages, enhanced benefits offerings, and an attractive work environment.

The Future of Work

> ▶ *Supply side (workers) at an Advantage – Demand side (employers) at a Disadvantage in this scenario.*

- Where there is a lower volume of open jobs, it typically results in a higher number of prospective candidates. This provides an obvious advantage to employers, as employers will likely be attracting a greater number of qualified and potentially highly qualified candidates for their jobs.

> ▶ *Demand side (employers) at an Advantage – Supply side (workers) at a Disadvantage in this scenario.*

■ Observations:

- In the US, economic cycles have averaged 58.4 months (less than five years) since 1945 [126]. Our current economic cycle has continued for ten years, but economists have been predicting a downturn in the near future. Individuals that have entered the workforce during this past decade have experienced what has appeared at times a euphoria of exciting job opportunities. But, more than likely, "all good things must come to an end", and we will likely experience a cycle of bad news from a job opportunity perspective. Today, of course, national and regional economic cycles are becoming increasingly intertwined with ripples occurring throughout the globe.

There are several additional macro trends underway as well as evidenced in this research by the Brookings Institute and other institutions.

→ The Evidence:

- "One of the most striking social science findings of recent years is that only half of today's 30-year-olds earn more than their parents. Raj Chetty and his coauthors showed that rates of absolute mobility—that is, the share of children with higher inflation-adjusted incomes than their parents—

The Future of Work

declined from around 90 percent for children born in 1940 to just 50 percent for those born in 1984." [127]

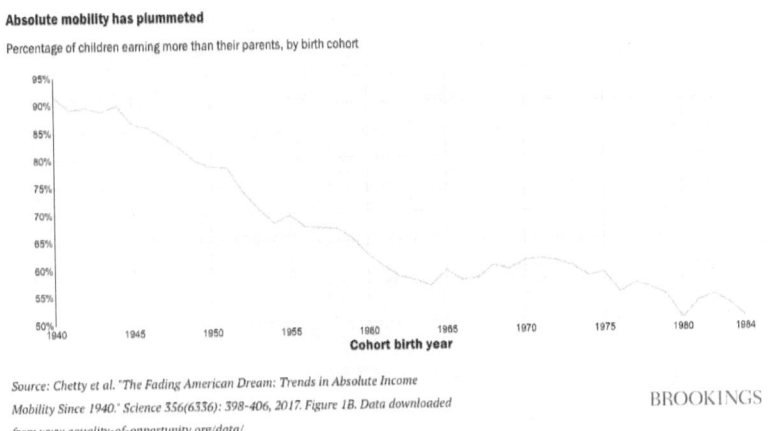

Source: Chetty et al. "The Fading American Dream: Trends in Absolute Income Mobility Since 1940." Science 356(6336): 398-406, 2017. Figure 1B. Data downloaded from www.equality-of-opportunity.org/data/

Source: Brookings Institute [128]

- "According to recent IRS data, more than 55 percent of adults ages 18 to 35 made under $25,000 annually. Just 9.5 percent earned more than $75,000. Though the younger people in the 18-26 set tend to work part-time and service jobs, more than 80 percent of these young millennials earned less than $25,000 per year." [129]
- "A recent study by Resolution Foundation found that income growth between generations in eight 'high-income' countries, including the United States, continues to slow. When Gen Xers reached ages 30-34, they saw a 30 percent income increase compared with the generation before, but millennials' income level at the same age fell by 4 percent in comparison with Gen X." [130]
- "Whereas baby boomers and the silent generation were almost certain (92 percent) to earn more than their parents, due to economic booms, increasingly accessible education and emerging industries, the study found that children born in the 1980s and beyond only have a 50 percent chance of attaining the same 'American dream' of economic mobility." [131]

The Future of Work

- "Millennials became the biggest U.S. generation this year, numbering some 73 million people. In terms of wealth, by contrast, they're still living in the shadow of previous generations. Despite making up nearly a quarter of the population, millennials — defined as those born between 1981 and 1996 — own a scant 3% of the country's wealth, according to the Federal Reserve's Survey of Consumer Finances. In comparison, when baby boomers were the age millennials are today (around 1989), they controlled 21% of all national wealth. Generation-X'ers at the same age (in 2004) held 6%. And it's not simply that millennials aren't amassing much wealth — they're also sinking deeper into debt, carrying a disproportionately high 16% of the nation's liabilities, the Fed data show." [132]

Certainly, in the United States we are experiencing an increased divide between those individuals that would be considered wealthy versus poor. I can only imagine that dynamics will also ultimately impact work and the workplace in a number of ways.

- "Since the 1970s the price of higher education has skyrocketed, putting the price of tuition out of reach for many low-income students. Over the same time, the tax code became more generous to the wealthiest Americans — the top marginal income-tax rate fell from 70 percent in 1980 to 39.6 percent in 2017, taxes on capital gains fell by more than half from the mid-1970s to the mid-2000s, and the estate tax has fallen as well. Those changes have made it easier for high-income Americans to grab more and more of the income pie in any given year." [133]
- "From 1980 to 2014, for instance, the bottom 20 percent of earners in the United States saw their after-tax income rise by just 4 percent, according to the World Inequality Report. By contrast, the top 10 percent saw their post-tax income more than double over the same period." [134]
- 'Western European countries, by contrast, took a different approach. 'Continental Europe meanwhile saw a lesser decline in its tax progressivity,' according to the report, 'while wage inequality was also moderated by educational and wage-

setting policies that were relatively more favorable to low and middle-income groups.'" [135]

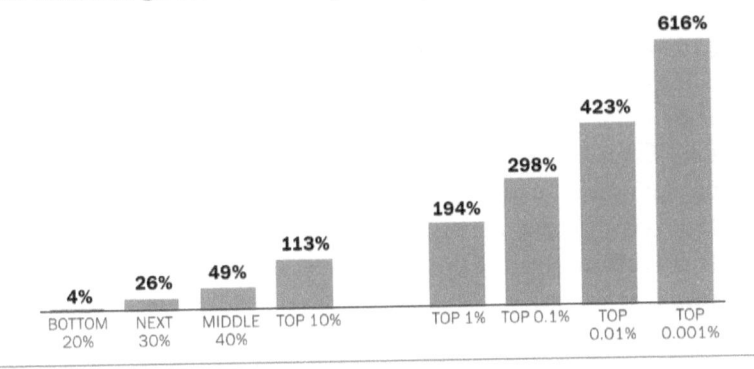

The rich get much, much richer
Post-tax income growth in the U.S. by income percentile, 1980 – 2014

Source: World Inequality Lab [136]

Another emerging trend, that tends to manifest at greater levels during economic downturns, is the impact that results from age discrimination on the senior workforce. The lack of recognizing, appreciating, and valuing decades of institutional knowledge continues to mystify me. Several articles on this topic caught my attention recently.

- "Age discrimination is an unfortunately common reality in the workplace, and its effects extend well beyond individual workers. According to a recent study by business insurance provider Hiscox, 21% of those over the age of 40 have been the victim of age discrimination in the workplace, 80% of whom say it has impacted their career trajectory." [137]
- "About three in five older workers (61%) have either seen or experienced age discrimination in the workplace" [138]
- "51 years old is the age at which workers believe they are most likely to experience workplace age discrimination." [139]

I imagine that economic cycles and economic issues will increase in complexity in the years and decades ahead and challenge at least a few economists and futurists with interesting employment opportunities. Yet one more likely important trend that will impact employment opportunities in the years and decades to come is the rise of the Gig Economy.

While the practice of hiring freelancers, contractors, consultants, and contingent workers is certainly not new, this tradition is steadily gaining more visibility. During the 1990s, companies like Microsoft were in the spotlight as they were hiring greater numbers of contract staff than employees. These companies were not providing their contractors with healthcare insurance and other employee benefits. More recently, there has been a lot of media attention on the millions of part-time contract rideshare drivers across the globe. Here is some additional background information on this topic.

- "The share of the U.S. workforce in the gig economy rose from 10.1 percent in 2005 to 15.8 percent in 2015" [140]
- "In 2016, 24 percent of Americans reported earning some money from the 'digital platform economy' during the previous year (2015). [141]
- "The number of self-employed individuals (many of whom are independent workers in the gig economy) soared by over 19 percent from 2005 to 2015." [142]
- "An internal document reviewed by the New York Times showed Google employs about 121,000 temporary, vendor and contract workers (TVCs) globally. This is while the company has 102,000 full-time employees, as of March. The Times found these employees are typically paid lower and have less comprehensive benefits packages than full-time staff. These roles span across all departments of the company, from chefs to coders." [143]
- "Google works hard to keep the 121,000 contractors it employs separate from its permanent employees. The two groups wear different colored badges, contractors are barred from some meetings, and they aren't provided employee perks such as health insurance and vacation time. The company apparently put these measures in place to make the status of its contractors as non-employees legally clear. Even

so, it's still risking a major labor lawsuit in Google's home state of California." [144]

- "One of the interesting ways that the aging workforce is changing the way we work is by bringing a measure of flexibility to the office. Companies are finding that employees in this age group require different work conditions. They are less interested in working long hours, less defined by their careers, and much more interested in part-time work. As a result of this trend, quality of life has become a key phrase—job sharing, part-time work, and flex scheduling can be partially attributed to this generation's influence." [145]
- "Research by the Insured Retirement Institute (IRI) also suggests trouble for some retiring Boomers. According to the study, 45% of Baby Boomers have no retirement savings. Only 55% of Baby Boomers have some retirement savings and, of those, 28% have less than $100,000. Thus, approximately half of retirees are, or will be, living off of their Social Security benefits." [146]
- "The share of companies offering older workers partial-year employment and shorter hours is expected to rise sharply. About 2 in 5 companies surveyed are considering offering part-time work or flexible hours by 2020, nearly double the current rate." [147]
- "Unfortunately, not all Gen Xers will continue to work full time. Many in the 'latchkey generation' are at a life stage that includes children, and some must care for aging parents, too. For these workers, workplace flexibility and work/life balance are critical components of the decision to stay in, or step away from, the workforce." [148]

There are numerous factors that have led to the rise of the "gig economy" which is essentially a labor market characterized by the prevalence of short-term contracts or freelance work as opposed to permanent jobs. In its earliest usage of this term, "gig" work referred to jazz club musicians in the 1920s. In October 2010, the software company Intuit initiated a study, "Intuit 2020 Report – Twenty Trends that will shape the next decade" [149] which included a projection that over the decade, the "study by Intuit predicted that by 2020, 40 percent of American workers would be independent contractors." [150]. The

The Future of Work

Financial Times has a good definition on the genesis of the "gig economy" term, "The phrase 'gig economy' was coined at the height of the financial crisis in early 2009, when the unemployed made a living by gigging, or working several part-time jobs, wherever they could." [151]

More recently though, this term has been in the news for a different reason. The rise of so-called unicorn companies such as Uber, Lyft, and Airbnb have resulted in a greater number of individuals starting to work this way. Some features, such as the fact that workers do not get healthcare, pensions or paid holidays, have hardly changed in the past few decades. What is new in today's gig economy is the way that technology has cast a wider net, drawing in people who would not otherwise be gigging at all. Think of the retired person who occasionally rents out a spare room on Airbnb, or the office worker who picks up an extra passenger on the morning commute through a ride-hailing app.

I had several opportunities to join the "gig economy" in the 2000s. I led two separate businesses that contracted part-time 1099 (US tax status for independent contractors) seasoned professionals on an hourly or per deliverable basis. I also launched an independent executive recruiting business in the height of the US Great Recession where I had the fascinating opportunity to interview hundreds of highly successful executives in their early 50s to mid 70s.

I encountered numerous real-life examples where it has become extremely challenging for executive-level professionals to land rewarding career opportunities in an age where the majority of employers appear to no longer value diverse and deep experience and prefer to hire employees with just several years' experience at considerably lower salaries. This trend has led many senior professionals to explore "gig economy" career opportunities as a means to bridge themselves to retirement. Quite often this has taken the form of launching an independent consulting practice with a heavy reliance on leveraging their personal professional network.

On a positive note, I have also found that gig jobs can be incredibly productive and rewarding insofar as there is typically very low, to no overhead as opposed to navigating a larger corporate structured

The Future of Work

environments and cultural norms. Working for yourself or independently can provide a greater personal satisfaction towards making an impact on a project or specific deliverable or delivering a service. It can also feel amazingly empowering to be in a position where you are 100% in control of your career and how, when, and where you earn a living.

The prevalence of the gig economy is now also gaining increased attention of state legislators especially in sight of the visibility of the new ride-hailing unicorns Uber and Lyft. While a vast number of consumers are taking full advantage of these new, very cost-effective services, many of the drivers may now be working for less than minimum wage in conjunction with not having access to employment benefit programs. Debates have been resurfacing regarding the support and benefits for contract workers versus employees. Recent actions include:

- "Gov. Gavin Newsom signed a controversial bill Wednesday [18-Sep-2019], known as AB 5, after months of uproar from businesses and gig companies like Uber and Lyft. The bill will require businesses to hire workers as employees, not independent contractors, with some exceptions. That will give hundreds of thousands of California workers basic labor rights for the first time." [152]
- "Uber, Lyft, and DoorDash have unveiled their ballot initiative to undo historic worker protections enshrined in AB5, California's new law that tightens the criteria for worker classification. The initiative claims drivers will receive a guaranteed pay equal to 120% of the minimum wage (that would be $15.60 in 2021, when the California minimum wage will be $13). Our review of the initiative leads to a very different estimate. After considering multiple loopholes in the initiative, we estimate that the pay guarantee for Uber and Lyft drivers is actually the equivalent of a wage of $5.64 per hour." [153]

The results of these debates and legislative actions will most likely have a considerable impact on millions of workers and jobs in the next several decades. This arguably strategic trend will also potentially have

The Future of Work

an extensive impact on workers across multiple generations from young to old.

As financial transactions continue to become increasingly digital, it will certainly have an impact on individuals that dispense, process, and handle cash including bank tellers, cash distribution (i.e. armored transport), and currency exchange businesses. The increased use of mobile payment and Near Field Communication (NFC) technology (i.e. Apple Pay, Android Pay, etc.) will also have a significant impact on the labor force in retail businesses across the globe.

- "Sweden has always been one of the first countries in embracing new technologies. There is a tradition in Sweden about being the first. This is noticeable throughout the Scandinavian country's history. And its financial system is not the exception. In 1661, Sweden was the first country in Europe to introduce banknotes. In 2023, Sweden is becoming the first cashless nation in the world, with an economy that goes 100 percent digital." [154]
- "In a report on mobile wallet adoption released earlier this month, Juniper Research estimated that consumer spending through digital wallets would rise 40% this year in North America and Europe to $790 billion in 2019. Juniper analysts said the increase is due to a continued migration from consumers using cash, the transition by major banks to contactless cards as well as a surge from millennials and younger consumers who are increasingly using the iPhone, where the firm estimates that one third of the devices are being used to make contactless purchases." [155]

■ **Reflections:**

This is another topic that has triggered several interesting reflections.

- To what extent will technological advances have an impact on our current historical economic trends in the future?
- What will be the impact on jobs and work in general from the potentially dramatic improvements in global healthcare

The Future of Work

through the impact of initiatives from institutions like the Bill and Melinda Gates Foundation [156], public agencies, and ongoing improvements from continued innovation – especially in third-world countries with sizable populations and high population growth rates?

- What would be the impact of major domestic policy decisions surrounding controversial topics like Universal Basic Income and income equality?

- What will be the ultimate economic impact of the global nationalism trends that has become popular across several continents in the past decade or so?

- While I have personally experienced and witnessed what I might refer to as "ageism" in the workforce, will this be a potentially more significant or less significant employment issue across generations in the decades ahead?

It appears to me that due to the result of several of the trends highlighted in this book that more individuals will be working in potentially multiple part-time positions throughout his or her career. At the time of this writing, I believe the "jury is still out" though regarding whether part-time positions will continue to be classified as independent contractors or employees that can take advantage of employment benefits.

The Future of Work

The Future of Work

DISMANTLING THE CORPORATE LADDER

"If the ladder is not leaning against the right wall, every step we take just gets us to the wrong place faster."

— Stephen Covey

Upon earning my bachelor's degree several decades ago, I was accepted into a two-year management program with a large global Fortune 50 corporation. I envisioned at that time that I would study hard, work hard, and enjoy a successful and satisfying career through earning my way up their corporate leadership ladder step by step. Ideally, I imagined, at some point in my 60s I would elect to retire from the same company and, with some luck, enjoy life as a retiree for another couple of decades with a corporate pension and a 401k plan that I had been funding consistently for 40+ years. I was on that track and climbing the ladder for over 15 years but decided to take a left turn and explore a different career adventure at that time. Many of my peer colleagues at that time though remained in the same company and department and eventually retired from the company.

It certainly appeared and felt like my career decision at that time in the early 1990s was the exception to the corporate norm. The following statistics from the US Bureau of Labor Statistics along with the increased velocity of CxO transitions truly reinforce to me that things have changed considerably over the past several generations.

→ **The Evidence:**

- "The median number of years that wage and salary workers had been with their current employer was 4.2 years in January 2018, unchanged from the median in January 2016" [157]
- "Generally, median employee tenure was higher among older workers than younger ones. For example, the median tenure of workers ages 55 to 64 (10.1 years) was more than three times that of workers ages 25 to 34 (2.8 years). Also, a larger proportion of older workers than younger workers had 10

years or more of tenure. For example, 57 percent of workers ages 60 to 64 were employed for at least 10 years with their current employer in January 2018, compared with 12 percent of those ages 30 to 34." [158]
- "In the past five years, CEOs transitions have become more common than they had been in the preceding five years. As a result, median tenure has fallen a full year since 2013." [159]

As I noted previously, the book "The 100-Year Life – Living and Working in an Age of Longevity" by Lynda Gratton and Andrew Scott was the genesis on my deep dive in 2019 to explore and contemplate the Future of Work. Upon pondering the impact of extending the life of a professional career by up to 50 percent from today's expectations in conjunction with the notion of a multi-stage life, it caused me to reflect on the concept of the "Corporate Ladder". I have subsequently concluded that the paradigm of climbing the "Corporate Ladder" will need to be revisited and potentially reinvented. My current thoughts on this topic include:

- **Observations:**

  - I suspect that relatively few Digital Natives today are joining companies early in their career and envisioning that they will retire from the same organization 40, 50, or even 60 years later.

  - I agree with the conclusions from the "100-Year Life" authors that couples may simultaneously elect to temporarily leaving the workforce to raise children in their mid-30s – or potentially early-40s due to continuing innovations in medicine and healthcare – after a 15 to 20 year initial career choice.

  - As noted earlier, the pace of technological innovation will continue to accelerate making it increasingly difficult to predict and anticipate career options in the next five years and beyond.

The Future of Work

- Due to numerous factors previously outlined, business lifecycles may also continue to collapse increasing the uncertainty of career and job options in the years beyond – especially with the same company and most likely along the same career path.

What triggered me to invest time to contemplate the future of the traditional "Corporate Ladder" paradigm is the amalgamation of each of the trends that I have noted previously. In a professional career environment where uncertainty rules, company lifecycles continue to shrink, jobs are continually being reinvented, future skills requirements are unknown, and workers envision their "careers" in a multi-stage perspective. These types of questions are front of mind as I try to envision what "work" is in the decades ahead.

■ Reflections:

- Do businesses and institutions continue to invest in their employees to enhance strategic soft skills including leadership if the concept of company loyalty no longer exists?

- Does the Gig Economy business model continue to expand where workers are primarily retained for a specific skill or deliverable for a period of time?

- Will workers, employers, or our local, state, or federal governmental institutions have the responsibility for the cost of continuing education and skills training for workers?

- In an extremely dynamic work environment, does the concept of leadership get redefined? Are employers going to assume that people are born with leadership skills and/or do institutions continue to invest in leadership training?

I honestly do not have the answers to the questions and will certainly be monitoring the insights and responses to these questions and many more during the decades ahead. If workplaces, from an employment perspective, are increasingly dynamic, I envision this potential dilemma as a crucial challenge for institutions of all shapes and sizes across all industries.

The Future of Work

REDEFINING THE CONCEPT OF A CAREER

*"Hide not your talents, they for use were made,
What's a sundial in the shade?"*

— Benjamin Franklin

"Prediction is very difficult, especially about the future."

— Niels Bohr

While you can certainly find predictions of various career opportunities that will be available in the next ten to fifteen years, I believe that the majority of us only have a vague idea on what those career options may be, let alone how to prepare for them. I assume that there will undoubtedly be career options in healthcare, science, engineering, public and social services, etc. – but I anticipate that the job descriptions will be considerably different than they are today.

I also suspect that jobs will continue to exist for trades skills in construction and manufacturing but imagine that the quantity of these job openings will likely be impacted by technological advancements and most certainly the skills required will change over time. Several of these projections have caused me to reflect on the challenges to predict career options that will be available to the next generation of workers in the early 2030s and beyond. Additional outlooks include:

➔ **The Evidence:**

- "According to a report published by Dell Technologies and authored by the Institute For The Future (IFTF) and a panel of 20 tech, business and academic experts from around the world, states that 85 percent of the jobs that will exist in 2030 haven't even been invented yet". [160]
- "By 2025, we'll lose over five million jobs to automation. However, there will also be a vast array of new jobs available

to university graduates - mostly related to knowledge creation and innovation." [161]
- "In 11 years' time, the year 2030, it's highly likely you'll be working in a job that doesn't even exist yet – and no, we're not talking about building flying cars or developing the world's first time machine. The world of work is evolving quickly, which means you have to figure out how to prepare for a future job role that's impossible to predict." [162]
- "As a student, your focus was primarily on the short term, but now you need a different set of navigational skills, to the far-horizon goals you will begin to orient your life toward. The average American has seven jobs over the course of their twenties. A third of recent college graduates are unemployed, underemployed, or making less than $30,000 a year at any given moment. Half feel they have no plan for their life…" [163]
- "The world will be short of 12.9 million health-care workers by 2035; today, that figure stands at 7.2 million. A WHO report released today warns that the findings – if not addressed now – will have serious implications for the health of billions of people across all regions of the world." [164]

The following chart from McKinsey Global Institute includes their projection on the impact of jobs by 2030:

The Future of Work

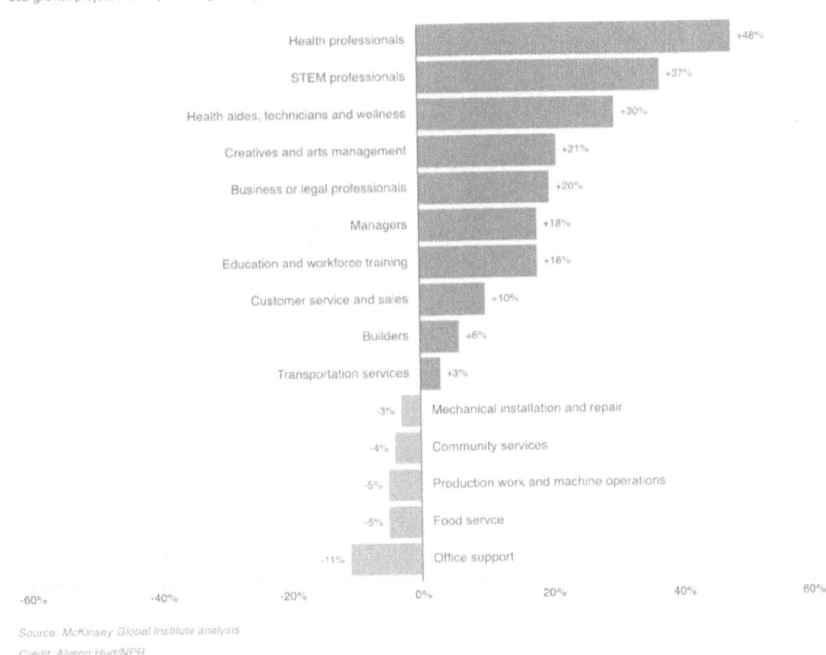

Source: McKinsey [165]

While there are a number of dire predictions regarding the potentially dramatic impact on careers and jobs in the coming decades, there are also many individuals that have a remarkably more optimistic view of work in the years ahead:

- "'Today there is a growing concern about whether there will be enough jobs for workers, given potential automation. History would suggest that such fears may be unfounded: over time, labor markets adjust to changes in demand for workers from technological disruptions, although at times with depressed real wages'. 'While advancements in machinery and technology may combine to provide graduates with the tools to explore, experiment and find interesting solutions to complex problems, they will also open up a world of new career opportunities.'" [166]

The Future of Work

As I highlighted in the previous sections, as you consider each of these trends collectively, it is increasingly challenging to predict and prepare for the future:

1. **Accelerated Business and Jobs Displacement**
2. **Demographic Shifts in the Workplace**
3. **Always-On, Always-Connected World**
4. **Reinvention of Higher Education**
5. **Changes in Generational Expectations**
6. **Global Economic Cycles and Trends**
7. **Future of the Corporate Ladder**
8. **Redefining the Concept of a Career**

So, as I contemplated all of these key trends collectively, it caused me to stop and further ponder this fundamental question:

■ **Reflections:**

- What will be the concept of a "career" be in say 2040 – and will the term "career" still be a relevant noun in the English language?

- Will our new work paradigm shift to anticipating that most people will have multiple careers throughout their life with the assumption that each "career" may only last a decade or two or even less than a decade?

Let me start by considering common definitions of the word "career" from several industry sources.

The Future of Work

ca·reer
/kəˈrir/
noun
an occupation undertaken for a significant period of a person's life and with opportunities for progress. [167]

career
ca·reer | \ kə-ˈrir \
noun
1: a profession for which one trains and which is **undertaken as a permanent calling** a *career* in medicine—often used before another noun
a *career* diplomat
2: a field for or pursuit of consecutive progressive achievement especially in public, professional, or business life [168]

career
/kəˈrɪər/
noun [C]
a job for which you are trained and in which it is possible to advance during your working life, so that you get greater responsibility and earn more money: [169]

Let's also consider the definitions of the common term, "profession":

pro·fes·sion
/prəˈfeSHən/
noun
1. a paid occupation, **especially one that involves prolonged training and a formal qualification.** [170]

profession
/prəˈfeʃ·ən/
noun
any type of work, esp. **one that needs a high level of education or a particular skill**: [171]

profession
(prəfɛʃən)
A profession is a **type of job that requires advanced education or training.** [172]

The Future of Work

You can easily argue, certainly in the short term, that many professions as we understand them today will continue to persist for at least the next few decades and potentially indefinitely. It appears obvious that the need for healthcare professionals will continue to exist. What I have attempted to stress though is that the skills and training for these professionals will definitely change along with the methods in how, when, and where these services are ultimately delivered. Nations will continue to need accountants and financial professionals to keep organizations accountable to their stakeholders, but undoubtedly these professions will continue to be disrupted due to the impact of new technological innovations.

I would venture to predict that factories are not going to operate, energy will not be generated, and physical products will not be created without some level of human intervention. The thousands of services that we depend on today are not going to disappear in a decade or two, but virtually all services will undergo disruptive change, and potentially even dramatic changes beyond our imagination today.

As I assess all the potential factors that will impact to greater or lesser degrees the "Future of Work", these additional questions arise to top of mind:

■ **Reflections:**

- What is the future of a career as a sales professional with increasingly ubiquitous access to vast amounts of information along with process automation? Will the sales profession, i.e. nurturing and closing a sales transaction, ultimately be coalesced within the marketing function as we know it today?

- What is the future for professionals who have chosen or desire a career as a Financial Planner? Will the voluminous amount of information available instantaneously in combination with AI essentially eliminate the need to hire a licensed professional to manage your financial investments and retirement planning?

The Future of Work

- What career guidance do you provide to your children entering college and the workforce in the 2020s if we are uncertain of what types of jobs will be viable in the following decade?

- What should individuals prioritize and invest in from a personal development perspective in the next decade to remain viable from an employment perspective in the 2030s?

- With accelerated innovation in the sciences and technology disciplines; will doctors, surgeons, attorneys, scientists, researchers, academic professors, etc. continue to be required to invest seven to twelve years or more into their education before the "officially" joining the workforce?

- Instead of deciding on a "career" or "profession" in our late teens or early twenties, will individuals instead choose to learn a skill, a trade, or master a specific area of knowledge to apply for the next few years and repeat this cycle potentially a dozen or more times throughout their professional life?

Bottom line is that I am convinced that no one, including our most prominent futurists along with my family members and current colleagues have a "Crystal Ball" that is providing them with keen insights into what career options, and more importantly, job opportunities will be available in the 2030s and beyond. At least for me, I find each of these macro trends intriguing – especially when you consider all of them concurrently in the context of jobs and careers.

Although I certainly had no grandiose plan or mission at the time, I have spent the vast majority of my career as a change agent and change leader in multiple industries and fields. What truly perplexes me as I investigate the concept of work is how employers and the workforce will continue to master and respond to the acceleration of change on careers and the workplace. Stay tuned, I think the evolution is going to be quite fascinating.

The Future of Work

The Future of Work

CONCLUSIONS AND RECOMMENDATIONS

"Change seems impossible—until it happens. At which point it seems to have always been inevitable."

— Beth Comstock ("Imagine it Forward")

"We always overestimate the change that will occur in the next two years and underestimate the change that will occur in the next ten. Don't let yourself be lulled into inaction."

– Bill Gates, "The Road Ahead", 1996

In this final section I will continue to analyze and contemplate the aggregate impact of the trends outlined in the previous chapters and focus on the impact of the challenges ahead on work and workforces specifically relative to:

1) **Individual Job Seekers**

2) **Employers**

3) **Recruiting and Talent Acquisition Professionals**

A frequently noted reference regarding the exponential growth and changes in computing technology is Moore's Law. Many professionals who have worked in the technology industry are familiar with this noteworthy projection named after Gordon Moore, co-founder of Fairchild Semiconductor and former CEO of Intel. Moore authored a report in 1965 [173] where he predicted that the number of components per integrated circuit would double every year as illustrated in the following rather detailed graph:

The Future of Work

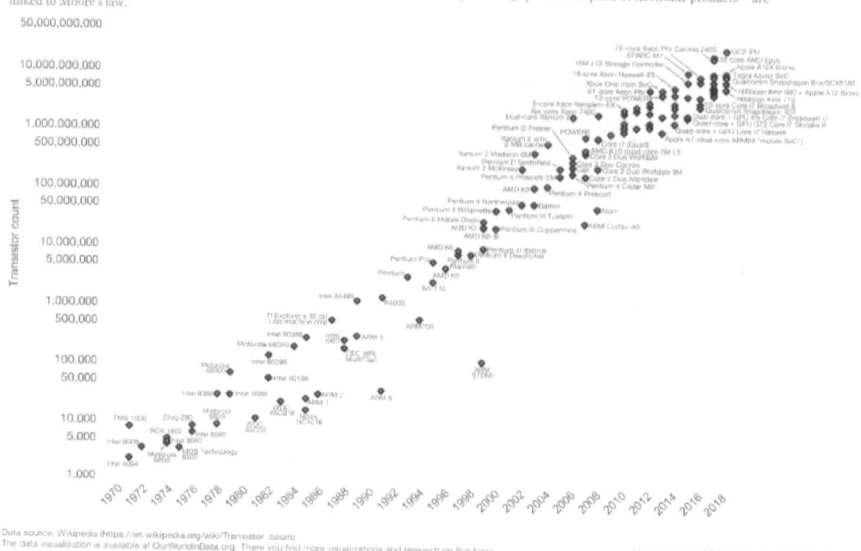

Source: Our World in Data [174]

Here are some interesting metrics that provide additional insight into our current digital world: [175]

→ **The Evidence:**

- "In 2014, there were 2.4 billion internet users. That number grew to 3.4 billion by 2016, and in 2017 300 million internet users were added. As of June 2019, there are now over 4.4 billion internet users. This is an 83% increase in the number of people using the internet in just five years!"
- Over 3.5 Billion Google searches are conducted worldwide each minute of every day. That is 2 trillion searches per year worldwide. That is over 40,000 search queries per second!
- Worldwide over 100 million messages are sent every minute via SMS and in-app messages!
- 26 billion texts were sent each day by 27 million people in the US. That is 94 texts per day per person in the US in 2017.
- "The total number of business and consumer emails sent and received per day will exceed 293 billion in 2019, and is forecast

The Future of Work

to grow to over 347 billion by year-end 2023. The number of worldwide email users will top 3.9 in 2019, and is expected to grow to over 4.3 billion by the end of 2023. Over half of the world population uses email in 2019." [176]

As I have researched, analyzed, and contemplated each of these intriguing trends over the past several months, it has undoubtedly caused me to pause and reflect on my own personal experiences of how technology has transformed my own life. For example, here is a small sample that illustrate some of the changes that I have experienced during my lifetime.

Visual Media
- → B&W TV with 3 VHF channels
- → Color TV with UHF channels
- → Cable TV channels
- → Video Cassette Recorder (VCR)
- → Blockbuster Stores
- → Digital Video Disk (DVDs)
- → Netflix DVDs by Mail
- → YouTube
- → Netflix Digital Streaming

Audio Media
- → Stereo Record Players
- → Reel-to-Reel Players
- → 8 Track Tape Players
- → Cassette Tape Players
- → Sony Walkman
- → Compact Discs (CDs)
- → Audible Audio Books
- → Podcasts

Print Media
- → Magazine Subscriptions
- → Local Book Stores
- → Big Box Bookstores
- → Amazon
- → iPad & Kindle

Communications
- → Letters
- → Postal Mail
- → Typewriters
- → Land Line Phones
- → Pay Phones
- → Electronic Mail
- → Wireless Phones
- → Bag Phones
- → Instant Messaging
- → 2G Cell Phones
- → BlackBerry Phones
- → 3G Flip Phones
- → SMS Texting
- → Social Media Platforms
- → 4G Smartphones
- → Collaboration Software
- → 5G Smartphones

Computing
- → Mainframes
- → Timeshare Computers
- → Minicomputers
- → Networked Computers
- → Dedicated Word Processors
- → Desktop Personal Computers
- → Laptop Computers
- → Speech Recognition Software
- → Client-Server Computing
- → Internet Computing
- → Application Service Providers
- → Tablet Computers
- → Smartphones
- → SaaS (Cloud Computing)
- → Ubiquitous Smartphones
- → Big Data
- → Artificial Intelligence

Guidance for Job Seekers

It is not remotely obvious to me on the variety of job and career options that will be available in the years 2030, 2040, and 2050 and beyond. Based on my experience over the past five decades and as Bill Gates observed in 1995, "We always overestimate the change that will occur in the next two years and underestimate the change that will occur in the next ten". My personal "crystal ball" for the concept of

The Future of Work

work for Generation Alpha falls between these extremes, depending on the day of the week.

(a) Technology innovations may dramatically eliminate the majority of the jobs as we know them today.

(b) We are grossly over-estimating the impact that technology will have on our livelihoods and lives in general.

For those who may have the impression that many of us are over-estimating the amount and speed of change that we will face in remainder of this millennium, consider this statement in early 2001 by renowned futurist Ray Kurzweil:

- "An analysis of the history of technology shows that technological change is exponential, contrary to the common-sense 'intuitive linear' view. So we won't experience 100 years of progress in the 21st century — it will be more like 20,000 years of progress (at today's rate). The 'returns,' such as chip speed and cost-effectiveness, also increase exponentially. There's even exponential growth in the rate of exponential growth. Within a few decades, machine intelligence will surpass human intelligence, leading to The Singularity — technological change so rapid and profound it represents a rupture in the fabric of human history. The implications include the merger of biological and nonbiological intelligence, immortal software-based humans, and ultra-high levels of intelligence that expand outward in the universe at the speed of light." [177]

And if you have any doubts about Kurzweil's record on his extraordinarily bold predictions, keep this in mind:

- "Of the 147 predictions that Kurzweil has made since the 1990's, fully 115 of them have turned out to be correct, and another 12 have turned out to be 'essentially correct' (off by a year or two), giving his predictions a stunning 86% accuracy rate." [178]

The Future of Work

People and institutions including businesses, non-profit organizations, academic institutions (private and public pK-12 schools and high education colleges and universities), public sector agencies (federal, state, local, etc.) across all industries are going to have to become increasingly more:

- Adaptable
- Agile
- Anticipatable
- Flexible
- Foreseeable
- Nimble
- Proactive
- Resilient
- Responsive
- etc.

■ **Observations:**

Along with the traits noted above, I anticipate that individual job seekers are going to have to prepare to focus and invest in:

1. Discovering your passions and potential career interests that align with your strengths and competencies.

2. Investing time in continuous learning to remain relevant and agile.

3. Continuing to invest in professional networking as an integral element in your professional development.

4. Investing in becoming multi-talented throughout your professional career(s).

5. Paying attention to trends, particularly those that will impact your career and obviously, you personally.

6. Learning to accept and embrace uncertainty while getting comfortable and learning to adapt to situations outside of your "comfort zone".

7. Adapting to embracing change and technological advancements. It likely will not be necessary or required to be a "technology geek", but we all need to be cognizant of the evolution and impact of technology in the workplace, particularly your chosen profession.

8. Focusing on building and maintaining resilience to continuous change.

At times I personally feel that the act of "reading" of traditional media (i.e. books, newspapers, and periodicals) has become a lost art due to the proliferation and addiction effects of social media platforms; impact of digital media; and ubiquitous mobile devices and vast number of apps among other factors. I continue to value investing time daily into reading from a diverse variety of sources and genres which stimulates my own creativity and challenges me to explore and examine topics from many different and often new perspectives. As I noted earlier, I believe that a continuous focus on learning will become even more essential to remain relevant in the years and decades ahead.

Guidance for Employers

I have often used an analogy of a modern roller coaster ride to describe my own career – with their unexpected twists and turns, rapid accelerations and decelerations, and resulting in finding yourself suddenly and unexpectedly upside down. I can only imagine that business in general will be increasingly more complex, and more closely resemble a roller coaster ride, including how institutions effectively lead and manage their workforce. I believe that in order for employers to remain viable they will be required to:

1. Embrace technological innovations with an emphasis on technology specifically applicable to their particular business

model. It is vitally important though to not become enamored with technology for technology sake.

2. Enhance the ability to learn quickly from mistakes and/or sudden market and economic shifts (in other words being able to "see around corners").

3. Proactively deliver the requisite education, training, coaching, and mentoring to your workforce to maintain a competitive weapon for your business or institution.

4. Remain attentive and adapt continuously to new workforce generational differences.

5. Emphasize agility to remain competitive and relevant in your respective market.

6. Accelerate the speed of making challenging and vitally important strategic and tactical business decisions.

7. Quicken decision-making to exit strategies and businesses that are no longer relevant to your target client or customer base.

8. Focus on the enterprise's ability to embrace change, building institutional resilience across your organization, and leveraging change leadership as a strategic and competitive advantage.

I have studied how individuals and organizations respond to "change", particularly major change, for over three decades. In the early 2000s, I identified five "Change Leadership Imperatives" for leaders to proactively and effectively lead, manage, and respond to change. These imperatives include:

1. **Embrace Reality** – Investing the time to welcome, embrace, and strive to understand different perspectives and literally, the individual "realities" of the personnel impacted by the planning change initiative throughout the organization.

2. **Prioritization** – Recognizing the potentially numerous competing priorities across an organization and understanding that implementing a new way of doing things requires that the initiative is a priority for all individuals impacted across the institution or enterprise. It should be acknowledged and embraced as such consistently throughout the organization. It is also essential that all impacted teams are aligned in respect to the priority and goals of the change initiative.

3. **Communicate, Communicate, Communicate** – I cannot overly stress how important that frequent and consistent communications are required to successfully lead and implement major change initiatives across an organization. It is important to recognize that your colleagues are likely already dealing with information overload and quite often multiple competing priorities. Far too often I find that feeble attempts to communicate (i.e. minimum effort expended to check a box) result in just noise to many recipients. You should assume that your colleagues are already afflicted with attention deficit due to vast amount of information coming at them continuously from far too many sources. Please also note that individuals respond differently to different communication channels (i.e. email, text, memos, training manuals, face-to-face, meetings, webinars, social media, etc.). Utilize multiple communication mediums to increase and improve awareness and commitment throughout the organization.

4. **Execution** – This is arguably the most important element to consider in leading change and I have found that "execution" is most often the critical factor that separates great businesses and institutions from all others. World-class execution requires extraordinary and consistent discipline throughout the organization with clear expectations and a very high degree of accountability from each and every associate in the organization. Of course, execution also requires and assumes outstanding strategic planning, project planning, relevant

metrics and performance management, and leadership among other things in parallel.

5. **Institutionalization** – It has been my experience that this is a factor that far too many leaders overlook and far too many leaders often do not even recognize. I often refer to this challenge as leadership attention disorder – insomuch that leaders quite often shift their focus and priorities on to the "next" strategic idea or initiative long before the other critical change initiatives have been fully implemented and "institutionalized" or "established as part of a culture, social system, or organization" [179]. Far too many change initiatives are implemented about 80%, 90%, or even 95% complete – but the organization loses focus before the complete scope of the change is fully implemented to achieve the full benefits that the leadership had envisioned.

One of the key benefits from adhering to these five change leadership imperatives is to build institutional perseverance, or "continued effort to do or achieve something despite difficulties, failure, or opposition: the action or condition or an instance of persevering" [180] across your enterprise or institution. Based on my conclusions of the impact of the key trends that I have outlined impacting the future of work – institutional perseverance is going to be a crucial factor for organizational survival due to the constant acceleration of change that workers and the workplace will have to respond to.

One additional recommendation that I have for employers based on my experience throughout my professional career is on the priorities that leaders should place their attention, focus, and allegiance. For many decades, experts and authors have argued whether organizations should place that greatest emphasis on their customers, their shareholders, or their employees. My leadership stakeholder priorities include:

1. Focus on your **Employees** as your highest priority as delighted, satisfied, committed, and motivated employees will consistently produce, support, and cultivate raving;

2. **Clients [Customers]** who will in turn support and generate a sustainable and reliable business or institution where your;

3. **Shareholders** (partners, investors, Board of Directors, etc.) ultimately succeed as a by-product.

Of course, the Shareholders of your business or institution may in fact be the organization leaders. One additional key component of this strategy is to also consistently treat your:

4. **Suppliers [Vendors, Partners**, etc.] fairly and with respect through executing agreements where your suppliers, your organization, and your clients all win through conducting business transactions with transparency and unwavering integrity.

I believe that this approach is the foundation of a true Win-Win-Win business model where all key stakeholders succeed.

Guidance for Recruiting & Talent Acquisition Professionals

While the potential impact to workers and employers from the macro trends I have discussed will undoubtedly be quite dramatic, I envision that the most significant impact may ultimately be levied on recruitment and talent acquisition professionals. I can imagine that the technological impact on the recruitment process in the decade or two ahead will be similar to the impact on the supply chain industry beginning in the mid 1990s with the introduction of Internet-based technologies. During that period, remarkable disintermediation occurred to the processes, businesses, and people that touched products between the supplier and the customer or consumer. In other words, new innovative technologies were used to replace the "middlemen" between the "supplier" or manufacturer creating a product and the ultimate "buyer" who consumed the product. Consider this scenario:

→ **The Evidence:**

The Future of Work

- "It might initially seem strange that a hiring manager could complete the entire hiring process on their mobile platform without directly working with a recruiter. But the self-service phone app model has already begun to dominate in many other business functions." [181]
- "Because other business processes are shifting over to the self-service phone app model, the pressure on recruiting will be tremendous to do away with the disjointed hodgepodge of sorcerers, recruiters, and outside vendors and to transition to the future of recruiting. This will be dominated by this integrated self-service phone app that offers every hiring manager end-to-end full-cycle recruiting at their fingertips, 24/7. This app will interactively walk the manager through each step and decision of the hiring process. And in the end, it will provide an objective metric assessment of the result (i.e. the performance of the new hire). And it will provide the hiring manager with guidance on how to improve their performance for their next hire." [182]

This is certainly not a foregone conclusion as I envision that many recruiting professionals will continue to respond by reinventing themselves and adapting their value proposition to the changing workforce needs for prospective employers. As noted above, the ability to adapt and continue to stay relevant will also be mission critical for recruitment professionals in parallel with the impact to workers and employers.

■ **Reflections:**

- As I have noted throughout my discussion of each of these key trends, I believe that an individual's and an organization's ability to adapt to change with an emphasis on building resilience will be paramount in the decades and most likely a key barometer on how workers and institutions adapt.

- Is it possible that recruiting and talent acquisition profession may no longer exist through disintermediation of the recruitment process (i.e. it becomes the responsibility of the hiring manager)?

The Future of Work

- Will our notion of a "work week" potentially disappear due to continued advances in technology and automation?

- The passing of time is certainly one thing that is totally out of our control. What we can control is what we do with the time that we are given. Time becomes even more precious as the pace of change accelerates. It is an important personal decision for each and every one of us to determine what we do with the time that we have at our disposal.

▪ Closing Thoughts

There are vast amounts of cash in venture capital and investment bank funds that are chasing the next AI and/or novel technology start-up company that will become the next Silicon Valley, New York City, Sao Paulo, London, Frankfurt, Lagos, Cape Town, Singapore, Hyderabad, Shenzhen, Tokyo, or Sydney unicorn darling (i.e. $1 billion market valuation). Today, in major modern global economies capitalism continues to rule and provides the foundation for massive investments in innovative solutions that continue to fuel the pace of change. It is hard to image that the pace of change will ever cease to accelerate, period.

One of my deepest concerns is the potential to drive deeper divisions into the "Haves" – those that can embrace and adapt to potentially radical change – and the "Have Nots" – the remainder that are not able to productively engage in the new economic realities in the decades ahead. The debates surrounding this subject and related topics will likely become even more prevalent and dynamic during these next few decades. Here are two additional perspectives on our economic environment in 2019:

- According to Daniel Markovits, author of "The Meritocracy Trap" [183], "Absolute economic mobility is also declining—the odds that a middle-class child will outearn his parents have fallen by more than half since mid-century—and the drop is greater among the middle class than among the poor." [184]

The Future of Work

- According to Joseph Stiglitz, Columbia University Professor and Nobel Prize winner, "Long regarded as a poster child for the promise of free-market individualism, America today has higher inequality and less upward social mobility than most other developed countries. After rising for a century, average life expectancy in the US is now declining. And for those in the bottom 90% of the income distribution, real (inflation-adjusted) wages have stagnated: the income of a typical male worker today is around where it was 40 years ago. Meanwhile, many European countries have sought to emulate America, and those that succeeded, particularly the UK, are now suffering similar political and social consequences." [185]

I anticipate that this will continue to be an intensely debated topic during at least the next several decades, unfortunately with a widening gap in opinions.

Another interesting analogy occurred to me recently while reflecting on change and how it ultimately impacts people and organizations. I have had the opportunity to experience the both physical and emotional impacts from multiple serious hurricanes firsthand having lived in the southeast US for over two decades.

One hurricane in particular had a rather dramatic impact to our region in respect to the considerable damage inflicted in a very short period of time. With this particular storm, the "eye" of the hurricane passed directly over my neighborhood including my house. The initial bands of the hurricane that preceded the eyewall can be extraordinarily intense and damaging (i.e. the terrorism in the early 2000s through the "Great Recession" from 2007 – 2009). One of the eeriest experiences I have had was to witness the "eye" of a hurricane pass through and then the bizarre and intense "stillness" that follows the disastrous wind, rain, and flooding (i.e. economic recovery during the current decade). What is always in store though, is the back of the eyewall with additional fierce wind and precipitation, and while typically, not as powerful as the front of the storm – it can still inflict considerable damage (i.e. what is potentially ahead in the next decade).

The Future of Work

My point here is, just as when the eye of the storm is on top of you, and all is peaceful and good, it's likely wise to not become too complacent about what the future may hold. At the same time, worrying about things that you cannot change (i.e. prevent a hurricane from passing through) is not a productive use of anyone's time. Being thoughtful, informed, and proactive though, about the things that you can control is typically an extremely wise move. Change is inevitable and to the extent that you are at least able to see the signs and anticipate impactful new trends, you will be positioned to potentially embrace the next key trend as a new opportunity versus a challenge.

In conclusion, I am an eternal optimist by nature and often times to a fault. I am hopeful and understand there is little that I can contribute except my openness, support, and empathy to Generations Z and Generation Alpha family members, friends, colleagues, and acquaintances and at this time as I eventually exit my "traditional" or my personal Second Stage and enter whatever is in store for me and my generation in the years ahead.

I sincerely appreciate and am very grateful that you have invested your precious time to join me on this thought-provoking adventure regarding "The Future of Work". I certainly welcome your feedback and insights to educate and enlighten me regarding your experiences and perspectives on this topic. I also wish that you are successful in finding the wisdom to identify your own satisfying and fulfilling personal career journey or journeys in the decades ahead.

*"Come gather 'round people wherever you roam
And admit that the waters around you have grown
And accept it that soon you'll be drenched to the bone
If your time to you is worth savin'
Then you better start swimmin' or you'll sink like a stone,
For the times, they are a-changin'"*

— Bob Dylan ("The Times They Are A-Changin")

The Future of Work

About the Author

Jack Spain is a veteran business leader with extensive strategic planning, operations management, product management, marketing, business development, IT management, and people management experience primarily with and within technology-based organizations across multiple industries. His professional experience spans organizations of all sizes from launching multiple entrepreneurial start-ups to strategic leadership roles in early stage and growth businesses. He has also led 100+ member teams in global Fortune 500 public corporations. Spain's diverse industry experience includes heavy industrial, transportation, energy, facilities and maintenance management, e-commerce, IT research and advisory services, technology commercialization, executive recruiting, Software as a Service, and Artificial Intelligence in commercial, academic, and public sector institutions.

Spain previously published three books including "Operations Proficiency Model: A Path to Success for Educational Institutions" (2013); "A Prescription for SMART Growth for Small to Mid-Size Businesses" (2013); and "The IT Leadership Pyramid: Essential Leadership Imperatives for Leaders of Information Technology Organizations in the 21st Century" (2009) which are available in Amazon.com.

The Future of Work

The Future of Work

The Future of Work

The Future of Work

Endnotes

1 https://www.cnbc.com/2019/07/02/this-is-now-the-longest-us-economic-expansion-in-history.html
2 https://www.cnbc.com/2018/06/05/there-are-more-jobs-than-people-out-of-work.html
3 https://www.benefitspro.com/2019/01/08/the-baby-boomer-generation-is-starting-to-retire-a/?slreturn=20190313071928
4 https://www.brookings.edu/blog/up-front/2019/03/26/women-staging-a-labor-force-comeback/
5 Ibid
6 Daniel Kahneman, "Thinking Fast and Slow", p. 256 (2013)
7 https://recruiters.welcometothejungle.co/en/articles/the-100-year-life-living-and-working-in-an-age-of-longevity-by-lynda-gratton-and-andrew-scott
8 https://www.bizjournals.com/triangle/news/2019/11/05/transition-to-ai-will-be-brutal-for-many-companies.html?
9 https://www.cnbc.com/2017/08/24/technology-killing-off-corporations-average-lifespan-of-company-under-20-years.html
10 https://www.nber.org/papers/w24333.pdf
11 https://www.nber.org/papers/w23285.pdf
12 https://www.cnn.com/2019/11/19/business/heliogen-solar-energy-bill-gates/index.html
13 https://about.bnef.com/blog/battery-pack-prices-fall-as-market-ramps-up-with-market-average-at-156-kwh-in-2019/
14 Ibid.
15 https://fortune.com/2019/12/10/artificial-intelligence-hottest-job/
16 https://fortune.com/2019/11/19/artificial-intelligence-will-obliterate-these-jobs-by-2030/
17 https://www.npr.org/2019/12/05/783164944/delivery-only-the-rise-of-restaurants-with-no-diners-as-apps-take-orders
18 https://www.usbanklocations.com/bank-rank/number-of-branches.html
19 https://www.businessofapps.com/data/youtube-statistics/#1
20 https://www.forbes.com/sites/danafeldman/2019/08/21/netflix-is-expected-to-lose-us-share-as-rivals-gain/#2498e5066d67
21 https://www.statista.com/statistics/1047393/cbs-all-access-subscribers-us/
22 https://musicoomph.com/podcast-statistics/
23 https://sbecouncil.org/about-us/facts-and-data/
24 Ibid.
25 https://www.wfae.org/post/scott-galloway-have-we-let-tech-giants-monopolize-more-economy#stream/0
26 https://www.ted.com/talks/scott_galloway_how_amazon_apple_facebook_and_google_manipulate_our_emotions#t-67238
27 https://www.amazon.com/Four-Hidden-Amazon-Facebook-Google/dp/B07565MYD1/ref=sr_1_1?
28 https://www.wsj.com/articles/tis-the-season-for-surge-robots-as-holiday-hiring-finds-automation-11572255001?

[29] https://www.washingtonexaminer.com/opinion/end-the-robots-are-coming-for-your-job-panic
[30] https://fortune.com/2019/01/10/automation-replace-jobs/
[31] https://www.youtube.com/watch?time_continue=1&v=CDjIydvz5NQ
[32] https://prospect.org/labor/where-are-the-workers-when-we-talk-about-the-future-of-work/
[33] Michio Kaku, PhD, Professor of Theoretical Physics, City University of New York and author of The Future of Humanity: Our Destiny in the Universe, webmd.com
[34] https://www.telegraph.co.uk/news/2019/09/27/ai-facial-recognition-used-first-time-job-interviews-uk-find/
[35] https://www.slideshare.net/dlavenda/ai-and-productivity
[36] https://www.wsj.com/articles/historian-yuval-noah-harari-on-the-robot-revolution-1538057544
[37] http://www.ichakadizes.com/does-disempowerment-cause-crime/]
[38] https://www.ifow.org/news/2018/6/13/a-roadmap-for-the-future-of-work
[39] http://www.iftf.org/fileadmin/user_upload/images/ourwork/Tech_Horizons/realizing_2030_future_of_work_report_dell_technologies.pdf
[40] http://theemergingfuture.com/speed-technological-advancement.htm?
[41] http://theemergingfuture.com/speed-technological-advancement-twenty-years.htm
[42] http://theemergingfuture.com/speed-technological-advancement-fifty-years.htm
[43] https://www.benefitspro.com/2019/01/08/the-baby-boomer-generation-is-starting-to-retire-a/?
[44] https://www.brookings.edu/blog/up-front/2019/03/26/women-staging-a-labor-force-comeback/
[45] https://www.texasbabyboomers.com/who-are-the-baby-boomers/
[46] https://www.pewresearch.org/fact-tank/2018/03/01/millennials-overtake-baby-boomers/
[47] https://www.forbes.com/sites/stephenmcbride1/2017/08/30/boomers-are-turning-71-these-3-charts-paint-a-perfect-storm-it-will-set-off-for-investors/#276c3c3b5485
[48] https://sloanreview.mit.edu/article/the-corporate-implications-of-longer-lives/?
[49] https://www.tlnt.com/society-is-changing-what-the-future-of-work-will-be-like-are-you-preparing/
[50] https://recruiters.welcometothejungle.co/en/articles/the-100-year-life-living-and-working-in-an-age-of-longevity-by-lynda-gratton-and-andrew-scott
[51] https://www.dailymail.co.uk/news/article-6965565/With-living-longer-CAMILLA-CAVENDISH-asks-extra-years.html
[52] Ibid.
[53] https://www.longevity.technology/aging-not-playing-out-as-expected-its-better/
[54] https://www.cnbc.com/2019/10/23/millennials-need-to-save-an-huge-percent-of-paycheck-to-retire-at-65.html
[55] https://www.amazon.com/100-Year-Life-Living-Working-Longevity/dp/1472947320/
[56] http://www.100yearlife.com/the-challenge/

57 https://www.brookings.edu/blog/up-front/2019/03/26/women-staging-a-labor-force-comeback/
58 Ibid
59 https://www.bizjournals.com/bizwomen/news/latest-news/2018/12/why-americans-are-opting-out-of-parenthood.html
60 https://www.npr.org/2019/09/20/762056390/investors-may-prefer-companies-with-more-women-in-the-workforce
61 https://www.nytimes.com/2019/09/14/us/appalachia-coal-women-work-.html
62 https://www.wsj.com/articles/where-women-fall-behind-at-work-the-first-step-into-management-11571112361
63 https://wiw-report.s3.amazonaws.com/Women_in_the_Workplace_2019.pdf
64 https://www.mckinsey.com/featured-insights/gender-equality/women-in-the-workplace-2019?
65 https://pitchbook.com/news/articles/startup-nation-of-women-the-most-valuable-vc-backed-company-led-by-a-woman-in-each-state
66 https://www.amazon.com/Invisible-Women-Data-World-Designed/dp/1419729071
67 https://99percentinvisible.org/episode/invisible-women/?
68 https://www.washingtonpost.com/business/economy/for-the-first-time-ever-most-new-working-age-hires-in-the-us-are-people-of-color/2019/09/09/8edc48a2-bd10-11e9-b873-63ace636af08_story.html
69 https://www.washingtonpost.com/business/economy/for-the-first-time-ever-most-new-working-age-hires-in-the-us-are-people-of-color/2019/09/09/8edc48a2-bd10-11e9-b873-63ace636af08_story.html
70 https://www.npr.org/2019/12/05/784451583/despite-job-boom-more-men-are-giving-up-on-work
71 Ibid
72 https://www.pewresearch.org/fact-tank/2018/03/01/millennials-overtake-baby-boomers/
73 https://www.skillsurvey.com/resource/generation-z-in-the-workplace-ebook/ (page 2)
74 https://www.newsweek.com/2019/06/28/gen-zs-are-anxious-entrepreneurial-determined-avoid-their-predecessors-mistakes-1443581.html
75 https://www.pewsocialtrends.org/2018/11/15/early-benchmarks-show-post-millennials-on-track-to-be-most-diverse-best-educated-generation-yet/
76 https://www.pewsocialtrends.org/2019/01/17/generation-z-looks-a-lot-like-millennials-on-key-social-and-political-issues/
77 https://www.statista.com/statistics/296974/us-population-share-by-generation/
78 https://www.pewresearch.org/fact-tank/2018/03/01/millennials-overtake-baby-boomers/
79 https://interestingengineering.com/generation-alpha-the-children-of-the-millennial
80 https://www.tomsguide.com/us/5g-release-date,review-5063.html
81 https://3dinsider.com/wearables-statistics/
82 https://www.forbes.com/insights/intelligent-world-the-state-of-the-iot/#b7e295b0d63a
83 https://www.space.com/spacex-starlink-satellite-internet-service-2020.html

[84] https://www.cbinsights.com/research/5g-technology-disrupting-industries/
[85] https://www.pewinternet.org/2018/05/31/teens-social-media-technology-2018/
[86] https://blog.microfocus.com/how-much-data-is-created-on-the-internet-each-day/
[87] Ibid.
[88] https://research.udemy.com/wp-content/uploads/2018/03/FINAL-Udemy_2018_Workplace_Distraction_Report.pdf
[89] https://www.washingtonpost.com/business/2019/10/07/nine-days-road-average-commute-time-reached-new-record-last-year/
[90] https://www.manhattan-institute.org/html/6-forces-disrupting-higher-education-11273.html
[91] https://www.kauffman.org/currents/2019/09/rethinking-education-to-make-graduates-and-workers-future-proof?
[92] https://www.kauffman.org/currents/2019/09/rethinking-education-to-make-graduates-and-workers-future-proof?
[93] https://www.kauffman.org/currents/2019/09/rethinking-education-to-make-graduates-and-workers-future-proof?
[94] https://www.weforum.org/agenda/2016/01/the-10-skills-you-need-to-thrive-in-the-fourth-industrial-revolution/
[95] http://www.ichakadizes.com/the-problem-with-formal-education/
[96] https://businessnc.com/daily-digest/?
[97] https://www.epi.org/publication/the-class-of-2017/
[98] https://www.shrm.org/ResourcesAndTools/hr-topics/employee-relations/Pages/What-Happened-to-the-Promise-of-a-4-Year-College-Degree.aspx?
[99] https://nscresearchcenter.org/wp-content/uploads/CTEE_Report_Fall_2019.pdf
[100] https://www.washingtonpost.com/local/education/study-finds-fewer-foreign-undergraduates-in-us-colleges--the-first-drop-in-13-years/2019/11/16/f20bdffe-07e4-11ea-818c-fcc65139e8c2_story.html
[101] https://www.npr.org/2019/12/16/787909495/fewer-students-are-going-to-college-heres-why-that-matters
[102] https://ourworldindata.org/grapher/price-changes-in-consumer-goods-and-services-in-the-usa-1997-2017
[103] Ibid
[104] https://www.thebalancecareers.com/what-are-soft-skills-2060852
[105] https://www.thebalancecareers.com/what-are-hard-skills-2060829
[106] https://www.shrm.org/resourcesandtools/hr-topics/employee-relations/pages/employers-say-students-arent-learning-soft-skills-in-college.aspx?
[107] Ibid
[108] https://news.cengage.com/upskilling/new-survey-demand-for-uniquely-human-skills-increases-even-as-technology-and-automation-replace-some-jobs/
[109] https://news.cengage.com/wp-content/uploads/2019/01/Employability-PR-graphic.pdf
[110] http://www3.weforum.org/docs/WEF_Future_of_Jobs.pdf

The Future of Work

111 https://www.topuniversities.com/student-info/careers-advice/future-skills-youll-need-your-career-2030
112 Ibid.
113 https://www.crimsoneducation.org/us/blog/jobs-of-the-future
114 http://www.hbs.edu/managing-the-future-of-work/Documents/dismissed-by-degrees.pdf
115 Ibid.
116 Ibid.
117 https://www.npr.org/2019/07/11/740219271/will-your-job-still-exist-in-2030
118 https://www.statista.com/statistics/797564/number-of-people-working-in-coworking-spaces-us/
119 https://www.amazon.com/Principles-Scientific-Management-Frederick-Winslow/dp/1296500799/
120 https://www.kornferry.com/institute/when-less-may-be-more?
121 Ibid.
122 https://www.npr.org/2019/11/04/776163853/microsoft-japan-says-4-day-workweek-boosted-workers-productivity-by-40
123 https://www.96fm.ie/news/buzz/campaign-for-four-day-working-week-in-ireland-officially-launches/
124 Ibid.
125 Ibid.
126 https://www.cnbc.com/2017/06/27/op-ed-a-history-of-economic-cycles-suggests-a-recession-is-near.html
127 https://www.brookings.edu/blog/up-front/2018/07/25/fewer-americans-are-making-more-than-their-parents-did-especially-if-they-grew-up-in-the-middle-class/
128 Ibid.
129 https://www.bankrate.com/personal-finance/millennials-earning/
130 Ibid.
131 Ibid.
132 https://www.cbsnews.com/news/millennials-have-just-3-of-us-wealth-boomers-at-their-age-had-21/
133 https://www.washingtonpost.com/news/wonk/wp/2017/12/15/u-s-lawmakers-are-redistributing-income-from-the-poor-to-the-rich-according-to-massive-new-study/
134 Ibid.
135 Ibid.
136 Ibid.
137 https://www.fastcompany.com/90392948/the-insidious-effects-of-ageism-in-the-workplace
138 https://www.aarp.org/content/dam/aarp/research/surveys_statistics/econ/2018/value-of-experience-age-discrimination-highlights.doi.10.26419-2Fres.00177.002.pdf?
139 https://www.hiscox.com/documents/2019-Hiscox-Ageism-Workplace-Study.pdf
140 https://www.naco.org/featured-resources/future-work-rise-gig-economy
141 Ibid.

142 Ibid.
143 https://www.forbes.com/sites/johanmoreno/2019/05/31/google-follows-a-growing-workplace-trend-hiring-more-contractors-than-employees/#25bcb724447f
144 https://www.inc.com/minda-zetlin/google-contractors-employees-legal-risks-misclassification-california-law.html
145 https://www.thebalancecareers.com/retiring-boomers-affect-job-market-2071932
146 https://www.investopedia.com/articles/personal-finance/032216/are-we-baby-boomer-retirement-crisis.asp
147 https://www.chicagotribune.com/business/success/ct-biz-baby-boomers-retire-dollarsense-20190301-story.html
148 https://hiring.monster.com/employer-resources/recruiting-strategies/workforce-planning/baby-boomer-workforce-gap/
149 https://http-download.intuit.com/http.intuit/CMO/intuit/futureofsmallbusiness/intuit_2020_report.pdf
150 Ibid.
151 https://www.ft.com/content/b5a2b122-a41b-11e5-8218-6b8ff73aae15
152 https://www.vox.com/2019/9/11/20850878/california-passes-ab5-bill-uber-lyft
153 http://laborcenter.berkeley.edu/the-uber-lyft-ballot-initiative-guarantees-only-5-64-an-hour/
154 https://interestingengineering.com/sweden-how-to-live-in-the-worlds-first-cashless-society
155 https://www.mobilepaymentstoday.com/articles/mobile-payment-adoption-just-might-be-on-the-verge-of-a-breakthrough/
156 https://www.gatesfoundation.org/
157 https://www.bls.gov/news.release/tenure.nr0.htm
158 Ibid.
159 https://corpgov.law.harvard.edu/2018/02/12/ceo-tenure-rates/
160 https://www.linkedin.com/pulse/85-jobs-exist-2030-havent-been-invented-yet-leo-salemi/
161 https://www.crimsoneducation.org/us/blog/jobs-of-the-future
162 https://www.topuniversities.com/student-info/careers-advice/future-skills-youll-need-your-career-2030
163 https://www.amazon.com/Second-Mountain-David-Brooks/dp/0812993268/ref=sr_1_1?, p. 16
164 https://www.who.int/mediacentre/news/releases/2013/health-workforce-shortage/en/
165 https://www.mckinsey.com/featured-insights/future-of-work/jobs-lost-jobs-gained-what-the-future-of-work-will-mean-for-jobs-skills-and-wages
166 Ibid
167 https://www.lexico.com/en/definition/career
168 https://www.merriam-webster.com/dictionary/career
169 https://dictionary.cambridge.org/us/dictionary/english/career
170 https://www.google.com/search?

171 https://dictionary.cambridge.org/us/dictionary/english/profession
172 https://www.collinsdictionary.com/us/dictionary/english/profession
173 https://newsroom.intel.com/wp-content/uploads/sites/11/2018/05/moores-law-electronics.pdf
174 https://ourworldindata.org/technological-progress
175 https://blog.microfocus.com/how-much-data-is-created-on-the-internet-each-day/
176 https://www.radicati.com/wp/wp-content/uploads/2018/12/Email-Statistics-Report-2019-2023-Executive-Summary.pdf
177 https://www.kurzweilai.net/the-law-of-accelerating-returns
178 https://www.diamandis.com/blog/86-accuracy-rate-in-tech-predictions
179 https://www.collinsdictionary.com/us/dictionary/english/institutionalize
180 https://www.merriam-webster.com/dictionary/perseverance
181 https://www.ere.net/alert-recruitings-future-will-be-dominated-by-a-full-cycle-self-service-phone-app/?
182 Ibid.
183 https://smile.amazon.com/Meritocracy-Trap-Foundational-Inequality-Dismantles-ebook/dp/B07MGDKDQN/ref=sr_1_1?
184 https://www.theatlantic.com/magazine/archive/2019/09/meritocracys-miserable-winners/594760/
185 https://www.project-syndicate.org/onpoint/the-economy-we-need-by-joseph-e-stiglitz-2019-05?

The Future of Work